FOUNDATIONS OF COMPUTER ARCHITECTURE: UNVEILING THE DIGITAL UNIVERSE

Detailed Table of Contents

Chapter 1: Introduction to Computer Architecture

- ## The Essence of Computer Architecture

Computer architecture is the conceptual framework and set of fundamental design choices that define the organization, functionality, and performance of a computer system. It encompasses various aspects, including the design of the central processing unit (CPU), memory hierarchy, input/output systems, and interconnects. The essence of computer architecture can be understood by diving into its key components:

1. **Instruction Set Architecture (ISA):** This is a critical component that defines the machine-level interface between the hardware and software. It specifies the instructions that the CPU can execute, the format of these instructions, and the addressing modes available to access memory and registers. ISAs can be classified as Complex Instruction Set Computing (CISC) or Reduced Instruction Set Computing (RISC), based on the complexity and number of instructions.

2. **CPU Design:** The central processing unit is the heart of the computer. It consists of the control unit, arithmetic logic unit (ALU), and registers. The control unit manages the execution of instructions by fetching them from memory, decoding them, and coordinating the necessary operations. The ALU performs arithmetic and logic operations on data fetched from registers and memory.

3. **Memory Hierarchy:** Computer systems employ various levels of memory hierarchy to balance speed, capacity, and cost. This hierarchy typically includes registers (fastest but smallest), cache memory (small and fast), main memory (larger and slower), and secondary storage (even larger and slower). Caching techniques are crucial to bridge the speed gap between different memory levels.

4. **Pipelining and Superscalar Execution:** To enhance CPU throughput, pipelines are used to break down the instruction execution process into stages. Each stage can work on a different instruction concurrently. Superscalar architectures take this further by allowing the execution of multiple instructions per clock cycle, exploiting both instruction-level parallelism and pipelining.

5. **Parallelism and Multicore Processors:** With the limitations of increasing clock speeds due to power and heat constraints, modern processors incorporate multiple cores on a single chip. This allows for increased parallelism, as multiple threads or tasks can be executed simultaneously. Efficient parallelism requires careful consideration of memory sharing, synchronization, and load balancing.

6. **Input/Output Systems:** Computer systems interact with the external world through I/O systems. These include interfaces for communication with peripherals, such as keyboards, displays, storage devices, and network interfaces. Efficient I/O handling involves techniques like memory-mapped I/O and direct memory access (DMA) to minimize CPU involvement in data transfers.

7. **Interconnects and Buses:** Interconnects are the pathways that facilitate communication between various components within a computer system. Buses are shared communication channels that connect the CPU, memory, and I/O devices. System performance heavily relies on the bandwidth and latency of these interconnects.

8. **Virtual Memory and Address Translation:** Virtual memory allows a computer to use more memory than physically available by utilizing disk space as an extension of RAM. Address translation mechanisms convert virtual addresses used by software into physical addresses in memory. This abstraction simplifies memory management for both the operating system and applications.

9. **Power Efficiency and Cooling:** As computer systems become more powerful, managing power consumption and heat generation becomes crucial. Power-efficient designs, dynamic voltage and frequency scaling, and sophisticated cooling solutions are employed to ensure reliable and sustainable operation.

10. **Performance Evaluation and Optimization:** Architects and engineers continually analyse and optimize computer architecture designs for better performance. This involves techniques like benchmarking, profiling, and simulation to identify bottlenecks and areas for improvement.

In essence, computer architecture defines the blueprint for designing efficient and effective computer systems. It balances trade-offs between speed, cost, power consumption, and scalability while considering the needs of both hardware and software components. Advancements in computer architecture drive the innovation and evolution of computing technology.

• A Historical Overview of Computing Devices

Let's take a journey through the history of computing devices, highlighting key milestones and examples:

1. Abacus (c. 2700 BCE)

The abacus, an ancient counting device, consisted of sliding beads on rods to perform arithmetic calculations. It was widely used in various cultures and is considered one of the earliest computing tools.

2. Antikythera Mechanism (c. 100–150 BCE):

The Antikythera Mechanism, an ancient Greek analog computer, was used to predict astronomical positions and eclipses. It is considered an early example of a geared mechanism capable of complex calculations.

3. Pascal's Calculator (1642):

Blaise Pascal created the Pascaline, a mechanical calculator with a series of gears and wheels, capable of adding and subtracting numbers. It was designed to help with arithmetic calculations.

4. Babbage's Analytical Engine (1837–1842):

Charles Babbage conceptualized the Analytical Engine, often considered the first general-purpose mechanical computer. It had an arithmetic logic unit, control flow, and memory, resembling modern computers. Unfortunately, it was never fully built during his time.

5. Hollerith's Tabulating Machine (1890):

Herman Hollerith's tabulating machine used punched cards to process and store data, primarily for census purposes. This approach laid the foundation for early data processing and automated calculations.

6. ENIAC (1945):

The Electronic Numerical Integrator and Computer (ENIAC) was one of the earliest electronic general-purpose computers. It was massive and used vacuum tubes to perform calculations. ENIAC was programmed using patch cables and was used for scientific and military applications.

7. UNIVAC I (1951):

The Universal Automatic Computer (UNIVAC) I was one of the first commercially produced computers. It introduced the concept of stored programs, allowing users to store instructions in memory for execution.

8. IBM 650 (1954):

The IBM 650 Magnetic Drum Data Processing Machine was one of the first computers to use magnetic storage for both instructions and data. It found use in business and scientific applications.

9. Transistors and Minicomputers (Late 1950s – 1960s):

The invention of transistors led to smaller and more reliable computers. DEC's PDP-1 (Programmed Data Processor-1) introduced the concept of minicomputers, which were smaller and more affordable than mainframes.

10. IBM System/360 (1964):

The IBM System/360 family of computers introduced compatibility across different models and marked a significant advancement in computer architecture. It laid the groundwork for modern computer systems.

11. Microprocessors and Personal Computers (1970s):

The development of microprocessors, such as Intel's 4004 and 8008, led to the creation of personal computers. The Altair 8800 and Apple I are notable examples of early personal computer kits.

12. IBM PC (1981):

The IBM Personal Computer, often referred to as the IBM PC, set a standard for personal computers. It was based on open architecture, allowing third-party manufacturers to create compatible hardware and software.

13. Macintosh (1984):

The Apple Macintosh introduced a graphical user interface and a mouse, revolutionizing the way users interacted with computers. It played a crucial role in popularizing graphical computing.

14. Laptops and Workstations (1980s – 1990s):

Advances in miniaturization led to the development of laptops and portable computers. Workstations, designed for advanced graphics and scientific applications, also gained popularity.

15. Internet and World Wide Web (1990s):

The creation of the World Wide Web by Tim Berners-Lee and the widespread adoption of the internet transformed computing into a globally connected environment.

16. Smartphones and Mobile Computing (2000s – Present):

The 21st century saw the rise of smartphones and tablets, combining computing, communication, and mobility. Devices like the iPhone and Android smartphones revolutionized personal computing.

17. Cloud Computing (2000s – Present):

Cloud computing emerged, enabling users to access and utilize computing resources remotely. Services like Amazon Web Services (AWS) and Microsoft Azure offer scalable computing power and storage.

18. Quantum Computing (Research Stage):

Quantum computers, still in the research and experimental stage, have the potential to perform certain types of calculations exponentially faster than classical computers using quantum bits or qubits.

This overview provides a glimpse into the evolution of computing devices, from ancient tools to modern computing paradigms. Each advancement built upon the innovations of the past, shaping the landscape of technology we experience today.

- ## Components of a Computer System

A computer system consists of various hardware and software components that work together to perform tasks, process data, and provide functionality to users. Let's explore the key components in detail, along with examples:

1. Central Processing Unit (CPU):

The CPU is the brain of the computer. It executes instructions and performs calculations. It consists of the control unit (manages instruction execution) and the arithmetic logic unit (performs arithmetic and logic operations).

Example: Intel Core i7, AMD Ryzen 9

2. Memory:

Memory stores data and instructions that the CPU needs to access quickly. It's classified into primary (volatile) and secondary (non-volatile) memory.

- **Random Access Memory (RAM)**: Provides fast data storage for currently running applications.

  Example: DDR4 RAM

- **Read-Only Memory (ROM):** Stores firmware and instructions needed for booting.

  Example: BIOS/UEFI chips

- **Flash Memory**: Used for non-volatile storage, like solid-state drives (SSDs) and USB drives.

  Example: Samsung EVO SSD

3. Storage Devices:

Storage devices provide long-term data storage. They include hard disk drives (HDDs) and solid-state drives (SSDs).

Example: Seagate Barracuda HDD, Western Digital Blue SSD

4. **Input Devices:**

Input devices allow users to provide data and commands to the computer.

- Keyboard: Enters text and commands.

  Example: Logitech G Pro X Mechanical Keyboard

- Mouse: Controls the cursor and interacts with graphical interfaces.

  Example: Razer DeathAdder Elite

- Touchscreen: Allows direct interaction through touch.

  Example: Apple iPad

5. **Output Devices:**

Output devices display information processed by the computer.

- **Monitor**: Displays visual output.

  Example: Dell UltraSharp U2719D

- **Printer**: Produces hard copies of documents.

  Example: HP LaserJet Pro

- **Speakers**: Output audio.

  Example: Bose QuietComfort 35 II

6. **Motherboard:**

The motherboard is the main circuit board connecting all components. It contains CPU sockets, memory slots, and peripheral connectors.

Example: ASUS ROG Strix B550-F Gaming

7. **Expansion Cards**:

These add-on cards enhance a computer's capabilities.

- **Graphics Card (GPU):** Handles graphical processing.
    Example: NVIDIA GeForce RTX 3080

- **Sound Card**: Enhances audio quality and features.
    Example: Creative Sound Blaster Z

8. **Power Supply Unit (PSU):**

The PSU supplies power to all components. It's measured in watts.

    Example: Corsair RM750x

9. **Cooling System**:

Cooling systems prevent components from overheating.

- **CPU Cooler**: Keeps the CPU temperature in check.
    Example: Cooler Master Hyper 212 RGB Black Edition

- **Case Fans**: Improve overall airflow within the computer case.
    Example: Noctua NF-F12 PWM

10. **Networking Components**:

Networking components enable communication over networks.

- **Network Interface Card (NIC):** Connects to wired or wireless networks.
    Example: Intel Gigabit Ethernet Card

- **Router:** Manages network connections.

Example: TP-Link Archer C7

11. Operating System (OS):

The OS manages hardware, software, and user interactions.

Example: Windows 10, macOS Big Sur, Linux Ubuntu

12. Software Applications:

Applications are programs that users run to perform specific tasks.

- Web Browser: Accesses the internet.

  Example: Google Chrome

- Word Processor: Creates and edits documents.

  Example: Microsoft Word

- Image Editor: Edits and manipulates images.

  Example: Adobe Photoshop

These components work together to create a functional computer system capable of various tasks and activities. Each component contributes to the overall performance and capabilities of the system.

- Role of Computer Architecture in Modern Technology

Computer architecture plays a pivotal role in modern technology by defining the structure, organization, and operation of computer systems. It serves as the blueprint for designing efficient and effective computing devices. Here's a detailed look at the role of computer architecture in modern technology:

1. **Foundation for Hardware Design**:
   - **Central Processing Unit (CPU)**: Computer architecture specifies the CPU's design, including its instruction set architecture (ISA), number of registers, data paths, and control unit. This design determines the CPU's performance and compatibility with software. For example, the x86 and ARM architectures are widely used in PCs and mobile devices, respectively.
   - **Memory Hierarchy**: It defines how data is stored and accessed within the system, encompassing levels of cache, main memory (RAM), and secondary storage (e.g., SSDs and HDDs). The memory hierarchy's design directly impacts system speed and responsiveness.

- **Input/Output (I/O)**: Architectural choices dictate how data is exchanged between the CPU and peripherals, including ports, buses, and protocols like USB, HDMI, and PCIe. This ensures proper data communication and device compatibility. USB, SATA, and PCIe are examples of interfaces designed according to architectural principles to enable high-speed data transfer.

2. **Parallelism and Performance**:

- **Multi-Core Processors**: Computer architects design processors with multiple cores to exploit parallelism, allowing multiple tasks to be executed simultaneously. This design is crucial for handling modern, multitasking workloads efficiently. For example, Intel Core i9 processors have up to 18 cores, allowing for parallel execution of tasks, which is critical for tasks like video editing or scientific simulations.

- **Vector Processing**: Some architectures, like SIMD (Single Instruction, Multiple Data), enable efficient execution of operations on large sets of data. Graphics Processing Units (GPUs) are a prime example, used extensively for tasks like graphics rendering, scientific simulations, and machine learning. Real Life Example Are Graphics Processing Units (GPUs) from NVIDIA and AMD use this approach to accelerate tasks like rendering and deep learning.

3. **Energy Efficiency**:

- **Mobile Devices**: Architectural choices are tailored to meet the power constraints of mobile devices. Mobile CPUs and GPUs are designed to strike a balance between performance and power efficiency to prolong battery life.

- **Server and Data Center**: In the context of data centers, computer architecture focuses on power efficiency and scalability to handle the massive computational demands while minimizing energy consumption. Example Intel's Xeon processors and AMD's EPYC processors are designed for data center workloads, optimizing power consumption while delivering high performance.

4. **Instruction Set Architecture (ISA)**:

- **Software Compatibility**: The ISA defines the set of instructions a CPU can execute, ensuring compatibility with software written for that architecture. For example, x86-64 architecture maintains compatibility with legacy x86 software while offering 64-bit capabilities.

- **RISC vs. CISC**: Architectural choices include whether to use Reduced Instruction Set Computer (RISC) or Complex Instruction Set Computer (CISC) designs, impacting processor performance, complexity, and power consumption. ARM uses a RISC architecture for mobile devices, while Intel and AMD employ CISC architectures for desktop and server CPUs.

5. **Security**:

- **Hardware Security Features**: Modern architectures incorporate security features like hardware-based encryption, secure boot processes, and hardware firewalls to protect systems from threats and unauthorized access. Cloud providers like Amazon Web Services (AWS) and Microsoft Azure rely on scalable architectures to offer services to millions of users worldwide.

6. **Scalability and Customization**:

   - **Scalability**: Computer architecture designs enable scalability, a crucial feature for cloud computing, where data centers need to expand or contract resources rapidly to accommodate varying workloads.

   - **Customization**: Some applications require specialized hardware, such as AI accelerators (e.g., Google's Tensor Processing Unit) or cryptographic co-processors. Architects design these components to optimize performance for specific tasks.

   - **AI Accelerators**: Companies like Google (Tensor Processing Unit) and NVIDIA (NVIDIA GPUs) develop specialized hardware accelerators for artificial intelligence workloads, demonstrating how computer architecture can be customized for specific tasks.

7. **Innovation and Advancements**:

   - **Technological Advancements**: Computer architects drive technological advancements by exploring new paradigms like quantum computing, neuromorphic computing, and photonic computing. These endeavors push the boundaries of what's possible in computing.

8. **Economic Impact**:

   - **Cost-Effective Designs**: Efficient computer architecture can lead to cost-effective solutions, which is critical for widespread adoption of technology in various industries.

In summary, computer architecture is the cornerstone of modern technology, shaping the design and capabilities of computing devices from smartphones and laptops to data centers and specialized hardware. Advances in computer architecture continue to drive innovation, enabling the development of faster, more energy-efficient, and more secure computing systems to meet the evolving demands of the digital age.

Chapter 2: Digital Logic Fundamentals

- Binary Number System

The binary number system, often referred to as base-2, is a numeral system used in mathematics and digital electronics. It employs only two symbols, 0 and 1, to represent numeric values and data. Unlike the decimal system (base-10), which uses ten symbols (0-9), the binary system is fundamental to digital computing because it aligns with the two distinct states of electronic devices, such as transistors, which can be either "on" (1) or "off" (0). Here's a detailed explanation of the binary number system:

1. Binary Digits (Bits):

- Binary uses two digits: 0 and 1. These digits are also called bits.

- A bit is the smallest unit of digital data and can represent two possible states or values.

2. Place Value:

- Each digit's position in a binary number carries a specific place value, just like in the decimal system.

- The rightmost digit has a place value of 2^0, which equals 1.

- Moving to the left, each digit's place value increases by a power of 2: 2^1 (2), 2^2 (4), 2^3 (8), and so on.

3. Converting Binary to Decimal:

- To convert a binary number to decimal, you multiply each binary digit by its corresponding place value and then add up the results.

- Example: Convert the binary number 1101 to decimal:

  - 1 * 2^3 + 1 * 2^2 + 0 * 2^1 + 1 * 2^0 = 8 + 4 + 0 + 1 = 13 (in decimal).

4. Converting Decimal to Binary:

- To convert a decimal number to binary, you repeatedly divide the decimal number by 2 and keep track of the remainders.

- Example: Convert the decimal number 10 to binary:

  - 10 / 2 = 5 remainder 0

  - 5 / 2 = 2 remainder 1

  - 2 / 2 = 1 remainder 0

  - 1 / 2 = 0 remainder 1

  - Reading the remainders from bottom to top, you get 1010 in binary.

5. Binary Arithmetic:

- Binary addition and subtraction are similar to their decimal counterparts, but they operate with only two digits: 0 and 1.

- For addition, if the sum of two bits exceeds 1, you carry over to the next position.

- For subtraction, you may need to borrow from a higher position if the minuend is smaller than the subtrahend.

6. Binary Representation in Computing:

- In computing, binary is fundamental. All data, instructions, and processing within computers are represented in binary.

- Bytes, which consist of 8 bits, are commonly used to represent characters, numbers, and other data types in computer memory.

- Binary is used for tasks such as encoding and transmitting data in computer networks and digital communication systems.

7. Binary in Electronics:

- Binary logic is the foundation of digital electronic circuits. It is used to design and build processors, memory units, and other electronic components in computers.

- Transistors, which serve as the building blocks of electronic devices, are essentially binary switches: they are either in an "on" state (representing 1) or an "off" state (representing 0).

Understanding the binary number system is crucial for anyone working in digital technology, as it forms the basis for all data representation and processing in modern computing systems.

- ## Logic Gates and Boolean Algebra

Logic gates and Boolean algebra are fundamental concepts in digital electronics and computer science. They form the basis for designing and analyzing digital circuits and algorithms. Let's delve into these topics in detail:

Logic Gates: Logic gates are electronic devices or digital circuits that perform basic logical operations on one or more binary inputs (0s and 1s) to produce a binary output. These gates are the building blocks of digital systems and computers. There are several types of logic gates, each corresponding to a specific logical operation:

1. **NOT Gate (Inverter):**

   - Symbol: ∘

   - Description: It has a single input and negates (inverts) the input. If the input is 0, the output is 1, and vice versa.

markdown code

Input (A)	Output
0	1
1	0

2. **AND Gate:**

   - Symbol: ∧

   - Description: It has two or more inputs and produces an output of 1 only if all inputs are 1.

markdown code

Inputs (A, B)	Output
0, 0	0
0, 1	0
1, 0	0
1, 1	1

3. **OR Gate:**

   - Symbol: ∨

   - Description: It has two or more inputs and produces an output of 1 if at least one input is 1.

markdown code

Inputs (A, B)	Output
0, 0	0
0, 1	1
1, 0	1
1, 1	1

4. **NAND Gate:**

   - Symbol: $\overline{\wedge}$

   - Description: It is the opposite of the AND gate. It produces an output of 0 only if all inputs are 1.

markdown code

Inputs (A, B)	Output
0, 0	1
0, 1	1
1, 0	1
1, 1	0

5. **NOR Gate:**

   - Symbol: $\overline{\vee}$

   - Description: It is the opposite of the OR gate. It produces an output of 0 if at least one input is 1.

markdown code

Input (A, B)	Output
0, 0	1
0, 1	0
1, 0	0
1, 1	0

6. **XOR Gate (Exclusive OR):**

   - Symbol: $\underline{\vee}$

   - Description: It produces an output of 1 if the number of 1s in the inputs is odd.

markdown code

Inputs (A, B)	Output
0, 0	0
0, 1	1
1, 0	1
1, 1	0

7. **XNOR Gate (Exclusive NOR):**

- Symbol: ≡

- Description: It produces an output of 1 if the number of 1s in the inputs is even.

markdown code

Inputs (A, B)	Output
0, 0	1
0, 1	0
1, 0	0
1, 1	1

Boolean Algebra: Boolean algebra is a mathematical system that deals with binary variables and the operations that can be performed on them. It was developed by George Boole in the 19th century and is widely used in digital electronics, computer science, and logic.

In Boolean algebra, variables can have one of two values: 0 (false) or 1 (true). The primary operations in Boolean algebra are:

1. **AND (·)**: Represents logical multiplication. It returns 1 only if all operands are 1.

2. **OR (+)**: Represents logical addition. It returns 1 if at least one operand is 1.

3. **NOT (¬)**: Represents logical negation. It inverts the value of the operand.

4. **XOR (⊕)**: Represents exclusive OR. It returns 1 if the number of true inputs is odd.

5. **XNOR (≡)**: Represents exclusive NOR. It returns 1 if the number of true inputs is even.

Boolean expressions are constructed using these operators to describe logical relationships and conditions. These expressions are fundamental in digital circuit design, programming, and various areas of computer science.

For example, consider a simple Boolean expression:

css code

A AND (B OR NOT C)

This expression combines the AND, OR, and NOT operators to express a logical condition. Depending on the values of A, B, and C, this expression will evaluate to either 0 (false) or 1 (true).

Boolean algebra and logic gates provide the foundation for designing complex digital circuits, writing computer programs, and representing logical conditions and operations in various computational and engineering disciplines. They are essential tools in the field of digital electronics and computer science.

- ## Combinational and Sequential Circuits

Combinational and sequential circuits are two fundamental types of digital circuits used in digital electronics and computer systems. They serve different purposes and operate differently. Let's explore each type in detail:

Combinational Circuits:

1. **Definition:**

   - Combinational circuits are digital circuits whose outputs depend solely on the current inputs. In other words, the output at any given moment is determined by the combination of inputs at that moment, and there is no memory or feedback involved.

2. **Key Characteristics:**

   - Outputs are entirely determined by the current input values.

   - There are no internal storage elements (like flip-flops or registers) to retain past states.

   - Combinational circuits are stateless and do not have memory.

   - They perform fixed logic functions and do not perform sequential or time-dependent operations.

3. **Examples:**

   - Basic logic gates (AND, OR, NOT, XOR, etc.) are examples of combinational circuits. These gates take inputs and produce outputs based on their logical functions without any memory or feedback.

4. **Applications:**

   - Combinational circuits are used for tasks where the output is solely determined by the current input, such as in data manipulation, arithmetic operations, and logical comparisons.

   - Examples include adders, multiplexers, demultiplexers, and data encoders.

Sequential Circuits:

1. **Definition:**

   - Sequential circuits are digital circuits that include memory elements (typically flip-flops or registers) to store and propagate information over time. The outputs of sequential circuits depend on both the current inputs and the past states of the circuit.

2. **Key Characteristics:**

   - Outputs depend on both current inputs and the internal state of the circuit.

   - Sequential circuits have memory elements that store information from previous clock cycles.

   - They can perform time-dependent and sequential operations.

   - Sequential circuits can exhibit sequential logic behavior, which means that the order and timing of input events can affect the output.

3. **Examples:**

- Flip-flops, registers, and memory units are the primary components of sequential circuits. These circuits can include various combinations of these elements to perform complex tasks.

- Counters, state machines, and clocked digital systems are examples of sequential circuits.

4. **Applications:**

- Sequential circuits are used in applications where the current state and past history of inputs matter. They are crucial for tasks like memory storage, data sequencing, control systems, and state-based operations.

- Examples include memory units in computers, digital clocks, and microcontrollers.

Key Differences:

Here are the primary differences between combinational and sequential circuits:

1. **Memory:**

- Combinational circuits have no memory or storage elements, while sequential circuits include memory elements (flip-flops) to retain previous states.

2. **Output Dependency:**

- In combinational circuits, outputs depend only on current inputs.

- In sequential circuits, outputs depend on both current inputs and past states, making them time-dependent.

3. **Purpose:**

- Combinational circuits are used for operations that don't require memory, such as logical operations and data manipulation.

- Sequential circuits are used for tasks that involve memory, state changes, and sequential logic, like counting, timing, and memory storage.

In summary, combinational circuits are stateless and produce outputs solely based on current inputs, while sequential circuits incorporate memory elements and consider both current inputs and past states to produce outputs. The choice between these two types of circuits depends on the specific requirements of a digital system or application.

- ## Introduction to Digital Design Principles

Digital design principles are the foundation of creating electronic systems that manipulate and process digital signals represented as binary data (0s and 1s). These principles guide the design and implementation of digital circuits, ranging from basic logic gates to complex microprocessors and digital systems. Let's explore digital design principles in detail, with examples:

1. Binary Representation:

- **Principle**: All digital information is represented using binary digits (bits). Each bit can have two states: 0 or 1.

- **Example**: In a digital thermometer, the temperature reading is converted into a binary code, where each bit represents a specific temperature range. For instance, 0010 might represent 20°C, and 1101 might represent 13°C.

2. Digital Logic:

- **Principle**: Digital systems are built on logical operations such as AND, OR, NOT, and XOR. Logic gates are used to perform these operations.

- **Example**: A simple example is an electronic door lock that only opens when both the correct PIN (input) is entered and a physical button (input) is pressed simultaneously. This behavior can be achieved using an AND gate.

3. Combinational Logic:

- **Principle**: Combinational logic circuits produce output solely based on the current input values, with no memory or feedback.

- **Example**: An adder circuit takes two binary numbers as input and produces the sum as output. It doesn't remember past calculations; the output is determined solely by the current inputs.

4. Sequential Logic:

- **Principle**: Sequential logic circuits incorporate memory elements (e.g., flip-flops) to store information from previous states. Outputs depend on current inputs and past states.

- **Example**: A traffic light controller is a sequential circuit. It changes the traffic light signals in a specific sequence (green, yellow, red) based on a combination of current sensor inputs and past states.

5. Finite State Machines (FSMs):

- **Principle**: FSMs are used to model systems with discrete states and transitions between those states. They are a fundamental concept in sequential logic.

- **Example**: An elevator control system can be represented as an FSM. It has states like "idle," "moving up," "moving down," and transitions between these states based on user inputs and the current position of the elevator.

6. Karnaugh Maps and Boolean Algebra:

- **Principle**: Karnaugh Maps and Boolean algebra are tools to simplify and optimize combinational logic circuits.

- **Example**: When designing a circuit to detect even numbers (a binary number whose least significant bit is 0), you can use Boolean algebra to simplify the logic: **(A AND NOT B)**.

7. Digital Circuit Design Flow:

- **Principle**: Digital design follows a structured process, including specification, design, simulation, synthesis, and implementation stages.

- **Example**: When designing a digital thermometer, the process starts with specifying the temperature range, sensor type, and display. Designers then create a circuit, simulate it to verify functionality, synthesize the design into hardware components, and finally implement the thermometer device.

8. Clocking and Timing:

- **Principle**: Timing is critical in digital design, and clock signals synchronize operations in sequential circuits.

- **Example**: In a microcontroller, a clock signal ensures that the CPU, memory, and peripherals perform operations in a coordinated manner. It ensures that data is read from memory and processed by the CPU at the right time.

9. Digital Components:

- **Principle**: Various digital components, including flip-flops, multiplexers, demultiplexers, adders, and memory units, are used to construct complex digital systems.

- **Example**: In a digital camera, a memory unit stores captured images until they can be processed or transferred to another device.

10. Testing and Verification: - **Principle**: Rigorous testing and verification methods are essential to ensure the correctness and reliability of digital designs. - **Example**: Before a smartphone goes into mass production, it undergoes extensive testing, including functionality testing, performance testing, and user acceptance testing, to ensure it meets quality standards.

11. Moore's Law: - **Principle**: Moore's Law suggests that the number of transistors on a microchip tends to double approximately every two years, leading to increased computational power and decreased cost per transistor. - **Example**: Modern microprocessors, such as those in smartphones, contain billions of transistors, enabling high-performance computing in small, affordable devices.

Understanding and applying these digital design principles is crucial for designing efficient and reliable digital systems, from everyday consumer electronics to complex computer systems. These principles provide a structured approach to creating digital devices that meet specific requirements and constraints.

Chapter 3: Processor Design

- ## Von Neumann Architecture

The Von Neumann architecture, also known as the Von Neumann model or the Princeton architecture, is a fundamental computer architecture framework that forms the basis for most modern computers.

It was proposed by mathematician and computer scientist John von Neumann in the late 1940s.

The Von Neumann architecture consists of several key components and principles, which are detailed below along with an example:

Key Components of Von Neumann Architecture:

1. **Central Processing Unit (CPU):**

- The CPU is responsible for executing instructions and performing arithmetic and logical operations.
- It consists of the Control Unit (CU) and the Arithmetic Logic Unit (ALU).

2. **Memory Unit:**

- Memory stores both data and instructions. In the Von Neumann architecture, program instructions and data share the same memory space, often referred to as the "von Neumann bottleneck."
- Memory is divided into two parts: Program Memory (for storing instructions) and Data Memory (for storing data).

3. **Input/Output (I/O) Devices:**

- I/O devices, such as keyboards, mice, displays, and storage devices, allow the computer to interact with the external world.

4. **Control Unit (CU):**

- The CU fetches instructions from memory, decodes them, and controls the execution of instructions.
- It manages the flow of data between the CPU, memory, and I/O devices.

5. **Arithmetic Logic Unit (ALU):**

- The ALU performs arithmetic (addition, subtraction, multiplication, division) and logical (AND, OR, NOT, XOR) operations on data.

6. **Bus System:**

- Buses are communication channels that connect the CPU, memory, and I/O devices. They consist of the Address Bus (for specifying memory locations) and the Data Bus (for transferring data).

Von Neumann Architecture Workflow:

The Von Neumann architecture follows a specific sequence of operations when executing a program:

1. **Fetch:** The CPU fetches the next instruction from program memory using the address provided by the program counter (PC).

2. **Decode:** The CPU decodes the fetched instruction to determine its operation and operands.

3. **Execute:** The CPU performs the operation specified by the instruction using the ALU.

4. **Memory Access:** If the instruction requires data from memory, the CPU retrieves it from data memory or writes results back to data memory.

5. **Write Back:** If the instruction produces a result, it is stored in a CPU register or written back to memory.

6. **Update Program Counter (PC):** The PC is incremented to point to the next instruction in memory.

Example of Von Neumann Architecture:

Let's consider a simple example of a program to add two numbers stored in memory and then display the result on a screen:

1. **Memory:**

   - Address 1000: Instruction to load the first number into a CPU register (e.g., R1).

   - Address 1001: Instruction to load the second number into another CPU register (e.g., R2).

   - Address 1002: Instruction to add the values in R1 and R2.

   - Address 1003: Instruction to display the result on the screen.

2. **CPU Operations:**

   - **Fetch (Address 1000):** The CPU fetches the instruction to load the first number from memory into R1.

   - **Decode:** The CPU decodes the instruction and knows it needs to load data from memory address 1000 into R1.

   - **Execute:** The CPU fetches the data from memory address 1000 and stores it in R1.

   - **Memory Access:** None in this step.

   - **Write Back:** Data is written to register R1.

   - **Update PC:** The PC is incremented to 1001 to fetch the next instruction.

3. **The process continues with similar steps for subsequent instructions.**

This example illustrates how a program's instructions and data are stored in memory and fetched and executed by the CPU following the Von Neumann architecture's sequential execution model. It demonstrates the flow of instructions and data between memory, CPU, and I/O devices.

- ## Central Processing Unit (CPU) Components

The Central Processing Unit (CPU) is the brain of a computer, responsible for executing instructions and performing various data processing tasks. The CPU is composed of several critical components that work together to carry out these functions. Let's explore the main components of a CPU in detail:

1. Control Unit (CU):

- The Control Unit manages and coordinates the execution of instructions. It fetches instructions from memory, decodes them, and controls the flow of data between different components of the CPU.

- The CU generates control signals that regulate the operations of other CPU components based on the decoded instructions.

2. Arithmetic Logic Unit (ALU):

- The Arithmetic Logic Unit is responsible for performing arithmetic operations (addition, subtraction, multiplication, division) and logical operations (AND, OR, NOT, XOR) on data.

- It performs mathematical calculations and logical comparisons required by program instructions.

3. Registers:

- Registers are small, high-speed storage locations within the CPU used for temporary data storage during processing.

- Examples of registers include:

    - **Program Counter (PC):** Stores the memory address of the next instruction to be fetched.

    - **Instruction Register (IR):** Holds the currently fetched instruction.

    - **Memory Address Register (MAR):** Contains the address of memory locations for data read or written.

    - **Memory Buffer Register (MBR):** Temporarily stores data being transferred between memory and CPU.

    - **General-Purpose Registers (e.g., R0, R1):** Used for various computational and data manipulation tasks.

    - **Accumulator (ACC):** Often used for intermediate results in arithmetic operations.

4. Cache Memory:

- Cache memory is a high-speed, small-sized memory unit located within the CPU or very close to it.

- It stores frequently accessed data and instructions to reduce the time required to fetch them from the main memory (RAM).

- Cache memory operates on the principle of locality, where frequently used data tends to be stored in cache for faster access.

5. Clock:

- The CPU operates on a clock signal that synchronizes its activities and ensures that instructions and operations occur at specific intervals.

- The clock speed, measured in Hertz (Hz), determines how quickly the CPU can execute instructions. Higher clock speeds result in faster processing.

6. Bus System:

- The bus system consists of various buses that facilitate data transfer between CPU components and external devices like memory, input/output devices, and expansion cards.

- The primary buses include the Address Bus (for specifying memory addresses), Data Bus (for transferring data), and Control Bus (for transmitting control signals).

7. Floating-Point Unit (FPU, Optional):

- In CPUs designed for scientific and mathematical computations, a dedicated Floating-Point Unit is included.

- The FPU handles floating-point arithmetic operations, which are used for real numbers with fractional components.

8. Vector Processing Unit (Optional):

- In some specialized CPUs, a Vector Processing Unit is included for efficiently performing operations on arrays of data, often used in scientific and engineering applications.

9. Superscalar and Pipelining (Advanced Features, Optional):

- Some modern CPUs feature superscalar architectures that can execute multiple instructions simultaneously.

- Pipelining is another advanced feature where multiple stages of instruction processing overlap to improve instruction throughput.

These CPU components work in harmony to execute instructions, manipulate data, and control the flow of information within a computer. The CPU's speed and efficiency are crucial factors in determining a computer's overall performance.

- ## Instruction Set Architecture (ISA)

Instruction Set Architecture (ISA) is a fundamental aspect of computer design that defines the set of instructions a computer's central processing unit (CPU) can execute and the way in which those instructions are encoded. ISA serves as the interface between the hardware and software, allowing programs to communicate with the CPU and control its operation. Here, we'll delve into the details of Instruction Set Architecture:

Key Components of ISA:

1. **Instruction Set:** ISA specifies a set of machine-level instructions that the CPU can understand and execute. These instructions cover various operations such as data movement, arithmetic and logical operations, control flow, and I/O operations.

2. **Registers:** ISAs define a set of registers that are part of the CPU. These registers serve as high-speed, small-capacity storage locations for frequently used data during instruction execution. They include general-purpose registers (for various data manipulation tasks) and special-purpose registers (for specific functions like program counter and stack pointer).

3. **Memory Addressing Modes:** ISAs define how memory is addressed and accessed. This includes addressing modes like immediate (values embedded in the instruction), direct (explicit memory addresses), indirect (addresses specified indirectly), indexed (using an index or offset), and relative (addressing based on the program counter).

4. **Data Types:** ISAs specify the data types supported by the CPU. Common data types include integers (with various sizes), floating-point numbers, characters, and boolean values. ISAs define the size, format, and representation of these data types.

5. **Instruction Formats:** ISAs determine the format of machine instructions. Different instructions may have varying formats, including opcode (operation code) fields, operand fields, and addressing mode fields. The format influences how instructions are encoded in binary.

Examples of ISAs:

1. **x86 ISA:**

   - The x86 architecture, initially developed by Intel and now also used by AMD, is prevalent in personal computers and servers.

   - Example Instructions:

     - **MOV AX, 5**: Move the immediate value 5 into the AX register.

     - **ADD BX, CX**: Add the values in registers BX and CX and store the result in BX.

2. **ARM ISA:**

   - ARM architecture is widely used in mobile devices, embedded systems, and IoT devices.

   - Example Instructions:

     - **LDR R0, [R1]**: Load the value at the memory location pointed to by R1 into R0.

     - **ADD R2, R3, #4**: Add the immediate value 4 to the value in R3 and store the result in R2.

3. **MIPS ISA:**

   - MIPS architecture finds applications in networking equipment and gaming consoles.

   - Example Instructions:

     - **LW $t0, 100($s0)**: Load a word from memory location (addressed by $s0 + 100) into $t0.

     - **ADD $s1, $s2, $s3**: Add the values in registers $s2 and $s3 and store the result in $s1.

4. **RISC-V ISA:**

   - RISC-V is an open-source ISA gaining popularity in academia and industry.

   - Example Instructions:

     - **LW rd, imm(rs1)**: Load a word from memory location (addressed by rs1 + imm) into rd.

     - **ADD rd, rs1, rs2**: Add the values in registers rs1 and rs2 and store the result in rd.

Importance of ISA:

1. **Software Compatibility:** ISA ensures that software written for a specific architecture can run on compatible CPUs, promoting software portability.

2. **Hardware Design:** ISA influences CPU design, including the number of registers, instruction set, and execution units. Different ISAs have varying performance characteristics.

3. **Compiler Development:** Compilers generate machine code based on a specific ISA, affecting code optimization and generation.

4. **Performance:** The ISA can impact execution speed, power efficiency, and the ability to exploit parallelism in software.

5. **Software Ecosystem:** ISAs influence the development of operating systems, libraries, and software tools tailored to a particular architecture.

In summary, Instruction Set Architecture defines the interface between software and hardware in a computer system. It encompasses the set of instructions, data types, addressing modes, registers, and instruction formats supported by a CPU. Different ISAs cater to diverse application domains and play a vital role in determining the compatibility, performance, and software ecosystem of a computing platform.

- ## Control Unit and Microprogramming

The Control Unit (CU) is a crucial component of a computer's central processing unit (CPU) responsible for controlling the execution of instructions. It manages the fetch-decode-execute cycle of the CPU, ensuring that instructions are correctly fetched from memory, decoded, and executed. One way to implement the control unit is through microprogramming. Let's explore the Control Unit and Microprogramming in detail:

Control Unit (CU):

The Control Unit performs the following essential functions:

1. **Instruction Fetch:** The CU fetches the next instruction from memory, typically based on the program counter (PC) or instruction pointer (IP). The fetched instruction is placed in a special register called the Instruction Register (IR).

2. **Instruction Decode:** After fetching the instruction, the CU decodes it to determine the operation to be performed and the operands involved. This involves interpreting the opcode and addressing modes specified in the instruction.

3. **Execution Control:** The CU generates control signals that direct the operation of other CPU components, such as the Arithmetic Logic Unit (ALU), memory units, and registers. These control signals ensure that the instruction is executed correctly.

4. **Sequencing:** The CU maintains the sequence of instructions to be executed, ensuring that they are processed in the correct order. It updates the PC or IP to point to the next instruction after each execution.

Microprogramming:

Microprogramming is a technique used to implement the control unit of a CPU. In microprogramming, the control unit's behavior is defined by a microprogram, which is a sequence of microinstructions. Each microinstruction corresponds to a specific control action or operation within the CPU.

Here's a breakdown of microprogramming:

1. **Microinstruction:** A microinstruction is the smallest unit of control in microprogramming. It represents a single control action, such as enabling a register, selecting an ALU operation, or setting a flag.

2. **Microprogram:** A microprogram is a sequence of microinstructions that define the behavior of the control unit for a particular machine instruction. It specifies the steps required to execute an instruction, including fetching operands, performing operations, and storing results.

3. **Control Memory:** In microprogramming, a control memory (sometimes called a control store or microstore) stores the microprograms. It is a memory unit that holds the microinstructions. Each address in the control memory corresponds to a unique microinstruction.

4. **Control Unit Execution:** During the execution of an instruction, the control unit fetches microinstructions from the control memory based on the current state of the CPU, the opcode of the instruction being executed, and other relevant conditions.

5. **Control Signals:** Each microinstruction generates control signals that direct the operation of various CPU components. For example, a microinstruction may enable specific registers, configure the ALU, or set status flags.

Advantages of Microprogramming:

1. **Flexibility:** Microprogramming allows for easy modification and adaptation of the control unit's behavior. Changes can be made by altering the microprogram without affecting the CPU's hardware.

2. **Complex Instruction Set Architectures (CISAs):** Microprogramming is well-suited for implementing complex instruction sets, where a single machine instruction may require multiple microinstructions to execute.

3. **Simplifies Hardware Design:** It simplifies the design of the control unit by breaking down complex control logic into smaller, manageable microinstructions.

Disadvantages of Microprogramming:

1. **Slower Execution:** Microprogramming can introduce additional overhead as the control unit fetches and executes microinstructions, potentially slowing down the CPU compared to hardwired control units.

2. **Increased Hardware Complexity:** Implementing a control unit using microprogramming requires additional hardware components, such as the control memory, which adds to the overall complexity and cost of the CPU.

In summary, the Control Unit is a vital component of a CPU responsible for managing the execution of instructions. Microprogramming is a technique used to implement the Control Unit's behavior by defining a sequence of microinstructions stored in a control memory. While microprogramming offers flexibility and simplifies control unit design, it can introduce some performance overhead and additional hardware complexity.

Chapter 4: Memory Hierarchy and Organization

- ## Memory Technologies: RAM, ROM, Cache, Virtual Memory

Memory technologies are essential components in computer systems, serving various purposes in data storage, retrieval, and management. Let's explore the most common memory technologies in detail, along with examples:

1. RAM (Random Access Memory):

- RAM is volatile memory used to temporarily store data that the CPU and programs need for current operations.

- It allows for fast read and write operations, making it ideal for frequently changing data.

- Example: DDR4 (Double Data Rate 4) SDRAM is a type of RAM commonly used in desktop and laptop computers. It provides high-speed data access for running applications and the operating system.

2. ROM (Read-Only Memory):

- ROM is non-volatile memory that stores permanent data and instructions that cannot be altered by regular write operations.

- It typically contains firmware and boot code necessary to start the computer.

- Example: BIOS (Basic Input/Output System) in a computer's motherboard is stored in ROM. It initializes hardware components during boot-up and loads the operating system.

3. Cache Memory:

- Cache memory is high-speed volatile memory placed between the CPU and main memory (RAM).

- It stores frequently accessed data to reduce the time it takes to retrieve information from slower main memory.

- Example: L1, L2, and L3 caches in modern CPUs are examples of cache memory. These caches store data and instructions that the CPU is likely to need quickly, improving overall system performance.

4. Virtual Memory:

- Virtual memory is a memory management technique that uses a combination of RAM and secondary storage (usually a hard disk drive) to simulate larger memory capacity.

- It allows the operating system to run more programs and manage memory efficiently.

- Example: When an application requests more memory than is physically available in RAM, the operating system uses a portion of the hard drive as "virtual memory" to temporarily store data that is not actively being used.

5. Flash Memory:

- Flash memory is non-volatile storage commonly used in devices like USB drives, SSDs (Solid State Drives), and memory cards.

- It retains data even when the power is turned off.

- Example: NAND flash memory, found in USB drives and SSDs, provides high-speed data storage and retrieval. It is used for long-term data storage and system boot drives.

6. Hard Disk Drives (HDD):

- HDDs are non-volatile storage devices that use rotating disks to store and retrieve data.

- They offer large storage capacity but have slower access times compared to SSDs.

- Example: A typical desktop or laptop computer often includes an HDD as the primary storage device for data and applications.

7. Optical Discs:

- Optical discs, such as CDs, DVDs, and Blu-ray discs, are optical storage media used for distributing software, videos, music, and archival data.

- They are read using lasers, and data is written using a laser's heat.

- Example: A DVD containing a movie or a CD containing software is a common example of optical storage.

8. Magnetic Tapes:

- Magnetic tapes are sequential-access, high-capacity storage media typically used for data backup and archival purposes.

- They are less common today but still used in some industries.

- Example: Large organizations and data centers may use magnetic tapes for long-term data storage and backup.

These memory technologies serve different purposes and are used in various combinations to meet the storage and performance needs of modern computer systems. Understanding their characteristics and roles is crucial for designing and using computer systems effectively.

- ## Memory Hierarchy Levels: Registers, Caches, Main Memory, Storage

The memory hierarchy is a critical concept in computer architecture that organizes different types of memory storage in a hierarchical manner based on their speed, capacity, and cost. It is designed to optimize the performance of a computer system by providing a trade-off between speed and storage capacity. The memory hierarchy typically consists of the following levels, from fastest to slowest:

1. Registers

- Registers are the fastest and smallest type of memory in a computer system.
- They are located directly within the CPU (Central Processing Unit).
- Registers store very small amounts of data, usually in the form of binary values (0s and 1s).
- Their primary purpose is to store data that the CPU is currently processing or needs to process immediately.
- Registers are used for operations like arithmetic calculations and data manipulation.
- Access to registers is extremely fast, as they are built into the CPU itself.

2. Cache Memory

- Cache memory is the next level of memory in the hierarchy and is designed to bridge the speed gap between registers and main memory.
- It is typically made up of multiple levels, such as L1 (Level 1), L2 (Level 2), and sometimes even L3 caches.
- Caches store frequently used data and instructions from the main memory.
- Data in the cache is organized into cache lines or blocks.
- When the CPU needs data, it first checks if it's available in the cache (cache hit). If not, it retrieves the data from main memory (cache miss) and stores a copy in the cache for faster access in the future.
- Cache memory is much faster than main memory but is also more expensive and has limited capacity.

3. Main Memory (RAM - Random Access Memory)

- Main memory, also known as RAM, is the primary working memory of a computer.
- It stores data and instructions that the CPU needs to perform its tasks.
- RAM is larger than cache memory but slower in terms of access time.
- It is volatile memory, meaning that its contents are lost when the computer is powered off.
- Data in RAM is organized into memory cells, each with its unique address.
- Modern computers typically have several gigabytes (GB) or even terabytes (TB) of RAM.

4. Storage Devices

- Storage devices represent the lowest level in the memory hierarchy in terms of speed but offer the largest storage capacity.
- This category includes hard disk drives (HDDs), solid-state drives (SSDs), optical drives, and various types of non-volatile memory.
- Storage devices are used for long-term data storage, including the operating system, applications, documents, and multimedia files.
- Unlike RAM, storage devices are non-volatile, meaning data remains intact even when the computer is powered off.
- Access times for storage devices are significantly slower than RAM.

In summary, the memory hierarchy levels, from fastest to slowest, are registers, cache memory, main memory (RAM), and storage devices. This hierarchy allows computer systems to balance the need for fast data access with the cost and capacity constraints of different memory technologies. The goal is to minimize the time the CPU spends waiting for data by keeping frequently accessed data in faster and more expensive memory levels, such as registers and cache, while using larger but slower storage devices for long-term data retention.

- ## Cache Design and Memory Mapping Techniques in detail

Cache design and memory mapping techniques play a crucial role in the performance and efficiency of modern computer systems. A well-designed cache system can significantly reduce the time the CPU spends waiting for data from main memory or storage devices. Let's delve into the details of cache design and memory mapping techniques:

Cache Design:

Cache design involves making decisions about the cache's size, organization, replacement policy, and write policy.

1. **Cache Size:** The size of a cache is a crucial factor in its performance. Larger caches can store more data, reducing the frequency of cache misses. However, larger caches are also more expensive and may have longer access times. Cache size is typically measured in bytes or kilobytes.

2. **Cache Organization:**

   - **Direct-Mapped Cache:** Each main memory address maps to a specific cache location. This mapping is simple but can lead to conflicts if multiple memory addresses map to the same cache location.

   - **Set-Associative Cache:** Cache locations are organized into sets, and each memory address can map to any cache location within its set. For example, a 4-way set-associative cache has four cache locations in each set. This reduces conflicts compared to direct-mapped caches.

   - **Fully Associative Cache:** In a fully associative cache, any memory address can map to any cache location, providing the highest flexibility but requiring complex hardware.

3. **Replacement Policy:** When a cache is full, and a new item needs to be loaded, a replacement policy determines which item in the cache gets evicted. Common policies include Least Recently Used (LRU), Random, and First-In-First-Out (FIFO). LRU is considered one of the best policies but can be computationally expensive to implement.

4. **Write Policy:** Cache write policies dictate how writes are handled. Common policies include:

   - **Write-Through:** Data is written simultaneously to both the cache and main memory. This ensures data consistency but can be slower due to frequent memory writes.

- **Write-Back:** Data is only written to the cache. The main memory is updated when the cache line is evicted. This can be faster but may introduce complexity in maintaining data consistency.

Memory Mapping Techniques:

Memory mapping techniques determine how memory addresses are mapped to cache locations.

1. **Direct Mapping:** In a direct-mapped cache, each main memory address maps to a specific cache location. This mapping is achieved by using a portion of the address bits as an index into the cache. For example, a 16KB cache with 4-byte blocks might use the lower 14 bits of the memory address as the index.

2. **Set-Associative Mapping:** In set-associative mapping, the cache is divided into multiple sets, each containing a certain number of cache lines. A portion of the memory address is used as an index to select a set, and the remaining bits are used to select a specific line within that set. For example, in a 4-way set-associative cache, there are four cache lines in each set.

3. **Fully Associative Mapping:** Fully associative mapping allows any memory address to map to any cache location, offering maximum flexibility. It uses a comparison mechanism to determine if a requested memory address is present in the cache.

4. **Multi-Level Caches:** Many modern processors use multi-level caches, typically L1, L2, and sometimes L3 caches. Each level may use a different mapping technique and have different characteristics to balance speed, capacity, and cost.

5. **Virtual vs. Physical Address Mapping:** Some cache systems may use virtual addresses (as seen by the CPU) or physical addresses (actual locations in RAM) for mapping. Virtual addressing allows for better memory management but requires additional translation steps.

Effective cache design and memory mapping techniques are essential for achieving high-performance computing systems. These design decisions are often tailored to the specific requirements of the target architecture and use cases, with trade-offs made between speed, capacity, and complexity.

• Memory Management Unit (MMU)

A Memory Management Unit (MMU) is a critical hardware component in modern computer systems that plays a central role in managing and translating memory addresses between the CPU and the physical memory (RAM). The MMU is responsible for providing several essential functions related to memory management, security, and virtualization. Here, we'll explore the MMU in detail:

Functions of a Memory Management Unit (MMU):

1. **Address Translation:** The primary function of the MMU is to translate virtual addresses generated by the CPU into physical addresses in the system's physical memory (RAM). This translation is crucial for enabling the use of virtual memory, which allows programs to access more memory than physically available and provides memory isolation.

2. **Virtual Memory:** Virtual memory is a key feature made possible by the MMU. It allows multiple processes to run simultaneously, each believing it has its dedicated memory space, even though they share the physical memory. The MMU keeps track of these mappings and ensures that processes cannot access each other's memory.

3. **Memory Protection:** The MMU enforces memory protection by controlling access to different parts of memory. Each memory page can have specific access permissions (e.g., read-only, read-write, execute) associated with it. If a process attempts to access memory it is not allowed to, the MMU generates an exception or interrupt, preventing unauthorized access.

4. **Page Tables:** The MMU relies on page tables to perform address translation. These tables store the mapping between virtual addresses and physical addresses. The CPU generates a virtual address, which is used as an index to look up the corresponding entry in the page table, yielding the physical address. Page tables can be hierarchical or multilevel to efficiently manage large amounts of memory.

5. **TLB (Translation Lookaside Buffer):** To speed up address translation, the MMU often includes a small, high-speed cache called the TLB. The TLB stores recently used virtual-to-physical address mappings, reducing the need to access the full page table for every memory access.

6. **Address Space Isolation:** The MMU ensures that each process has its own isolated address space. This isolation prevents one process from accessing the memory of another, providing security and stability to the operating system.

7. **Virtualization:** In virtualization environments, such as virtual machines (VMs), the MMU plays a crucial role in mapping virtual addresses used by guest operating systems to the actual physical addresses managed by the host system. This allows multiple virtualized instances to run concurrently on the same physical hardware.

8. **Memory Protection Rings:** The MMU is often used in conjunction with CPU privilege levels, often referred to as protection rings or privilege levels (e.g., Ring 0 for kernel, Ring 3 for user mode). The MMU helps enforce the separation between these privilege levels, ensuring that user processes cannot access privileged kernel memory.

Address Translation Process:

The address translation process carried out by the MMU typically involves the following steps:

1. The CPU generates a virtual memory address during program execution.

2. The MMU uses this virtual address to look up the corresponding physical address in the page table.

3. If the mapping is found in the TLB, it is used directly; otherwise, the MMU retrieves the mapping from the page table in memory.

4. The physical address is then used to access the actual data in RAM.

In summary, the Memory Management Unit (MMU) is a crucial hardware component responsible for translating virtual addresses into physical addresses, managing memory protection and isolation, and enabling the use of virtual memory. It plays a vital role in modern computer systems by ensuring efficient and secure memory access for both the operating system and user applications.

Chapter 5: Input and Output Systems

- ### I/O Interfaces and Devices

I/O (Input/Output) interfaces and devices are essential components of computer systems that enable communication between the CPU (Central Processing Unit) and external peripherals or devices. These interfaces and devices facilitate data transfer, user interactions, and communication with the outside world. Let's explore I/O interfaces and devices in detail:

I/O Interfaces:

1. **I/O Ports:** I/O ports are hardware interfaces on a computer or microcontroller that connect to external devices. They are used for transferring data between the CPU and peripherals. I/O ports can be categorized as parallel (multiple data lines at once) or serial (one data line at a time). Common parallel ports include the GPIO (General-Purpose Input/Output) pins on microcontrollers, while serial ports include interfaces like UART, SPI, and I2C.

2. **USB (Universal Serial Bus):** USB is a widely used standard for connecting various external devices to a computer, such as keyboards, mice, printers, external hard drives, and smartphones. USB supports hot-swapping, which means devices can be connected or disconnected without turning off the computer.

3. **FireWire (IEEE 1394):** FireWire is an older interface primarily used for connecting multimedia devices, such as digital cameras and camcorders, to computers. It provides high-speed data transfer and is suitable for real-time multimedia applications.

4. **Ethernet:** Ethernet is a networking interface used for connecting computers and devices to local area networks (LANs) and the internet. It supports data transfer at high speeds and is commonly used for internet connectivity, file sharing, and networked applications.

5. **PCI/PCIe (Peripheral Component Interconnect/PCI Express):** These are expansion slots found on desktop computers and servers, used to connect various add-on cards, including graphics cards, network cards, sound cards, and storage controllers. PCIe is the modern and faster version of PCI.

6. **SATA (Serial Advanced Technology Attachment):** SATA is an interface for connecting internal storage devices, such as hard disk drives (HDDs) and solid-state drives (SSDs), to a computer's motherboard.

I/O Devices:

1. **Keyboard:** Keyboards are input devices that allow users to enter text and commands into a computer. They use various technologies, including mechanical switches and membrane keys.

2. **Mouse and Pointing Devices:** Mice, trackpads, and pointing sticks are used for cursor control and interacting with graphical user interfaces. These devices may use optical, laser, or touch-sensitive technology.

3. **Display/Monitor:** Monitors or displays are output devices that provide visual feedback to the user. They come in various types, including LCD, LED, OLED, and CRT displays.

4. **Printers and Scanners:** Printers produce hard copies of digital documents, while scanners convert physical documents or images into digital format. Common types of printers include inkjet, laser, and dot matrix.

5. **Storage Devices:** Storage devices, including HDDs and SSDs, are used for long-term data storage. External storage devices like USB drives and memory cards are also common.

6. **Network Adapters:** Network adapters (NICs - Network Interface Cards) enable wired or wireless network connectivity. Wi-Fi adapters and Ethernet cards are examples of network adapters.

7. **Audio Devices:** Audio input and output devices, such as microphones, speakers, and sound cards, facilitate audio communication and multimedia playback.

8. **Graphics Cards/GPUs:** Graphics processing units (GPUs) or graphics cards are specialized hardware used to accelerate graphics rendering and video processing tasks. They are essential for gaming and graphic-intensive applications.

9. **Webcams:** Webcams are video input devices used for capturing and transmitting video and audio over the internet. They are commonly used for video conferencing and live streaming.

10. **Controllers and Gamepads:** Game controllers, including gamepads, joysticks, and steering wheels, are input devices used for gaming and controlling applications that require precise input.

11. **Touchscreens:** Touchscreens are input and output devices that allow users to interact directly with the display by touching it. They are commonly found in smartphones, tablets, and interactive kiosks.

12. **Biometric Devices:** Biometric devices, such as fingerprint scanners and facial recognition cameras, provide secure and convenient authentication and access control.

13. **Sensors:** Various sensors, like temperature sensors, motion sensors, and environmental sensors, collect data from the physical world and provide input to computer systems.

These are just some of the many I/O interfaces and devices used in computer systems. The selection of interfaces and devices depends on the specific requirements and use cases of the computer or electronic system, and advances in technology continue to introduce new interfaces and devices to meet evolving needs.

- Polling, Interrupts, and DMA

Polling, interrupts, and DMA (Direct Memory Access) are three different techniques used in computer systems to manage I/O (Input/Output) operations and efficiently transfer data between peripherals and memory or CPU. Let's explore each of these techniques in detail:

1. Polling:

Definition: Polling is a technique in which the CPU continuously checks the status of an I/O device to determine if it is ready to send or receive data. It involves repeated and frequent CPU polling of the device's status register or flag.

Characteristics:

- **CPU-Intensive:** Polling relies heavily on the CPU's processing power, as it continually checks the status of the I/O device.

- **Deterministic:** Polling provides a deterministic response time because the CPU knows exactly when it checks the device's status.

- **Simple to Implement:** Polling is relatively straightforward to implement, making it suitable for simple embedded systems or scenarios with limited hardware resources.

- **Wasteful in Busy Wait:** Polling often involves busy waiting, where the CPU repeatedly checks the device's status, leading to wasted CPU cycles when the device is not ready.

Use Cases: Polling is commonly used in scenarios where simplicity and determinism are more critical than efficiency, such as simple microcontroller-based systems, low-level device drivers, or when interfacing with devices that do not support interrupts.

2. Interrupts:

Definition: Interrupts are signals generated by hardware devices or software to asynchronously notify the CPU that a specific event or condition has occurred and requires immediate attention. The CPU responds to interrupts by suspending its current execution and executing an interrupt service routine (ISR) to handle the event.

Characteristics:

- **Asynchronous:** Interrupts are asynchronous events, meaning they can occur at any time, even while the CPU is executing other instructions.

- **Efficient:** Interrupts are highly efficient because they allow the CPU to perform other tasks while waiting for events to occur.

- **Complex Handling:** Implementing interrupt service routines (ISRs) can be complex, especially for managing multiple interrupts and their priorities.

- **Prioritization:** Systems can prioritize interrupts based on the importance of events, ensuring critical events are handled first.

Use Cases: Interrupts are used in virtually all modern computer systems, from desktop computers to embedded systems. They are essential for handling external events like keyboard input, mouse movements, network activity, and hardware faults.

3. DMA (Direct Memory Access):

Definition: DMA is a technique that allows peripherals or I/O devices to transfer data directly to and from memory without involving the CPU in every data transfer. A DMA controller manages these transfers, reducing CPU overhead.

Characteristics:

- **Offloads CPU:** DMA significantly reduces CPU involvement in data transfers, freeing up the CPU for other tasks.

- **High Data Throughput:** DMA is ideal for transferring large blocks of data quickly, such as reading/writing from/to storage devices or memory-to-memory copies.

- **Complex Setup:** Configuring and managing DMA channels and buffers can be complex, especially in systems with multiple devices and memory regions.

- **Synchronous or Asynchronous:** DMA transfers can be either synchronous (initiated by the CPU) or asynchronous (triggered by external events or devices).

Use Cases: DMA is commonly used in scenarios where high-speed data transfer is required, such as disk I/O, audio processing, video streaming, and memory copying. It's also essential for managing data between system memory and various peripherals.

In summary, polling, interrupts, and DMA are different techniques used for managing I/O operations and data transfers in computer systems. Each has its own advantages and use cases, and the choice of technique depends on factors such as system requirements, hardware capabilities, and the need for efficiency and responsiveness.

- ## I/O Communication Methods

I/O (Input/Output) communication methods refer to the ways in which data is exchanged between a computer or microcontroller and external devices or peripherals. These methods vary in complexity, speed, and suitability for different applications. Here, we'll explore several I/O communication methods in detail:

1. Serial Communication:

- **Definition:** Serial communication involves sending and receiving data one bit at a time over a single wire (serial line). It is commonly used when devices are relatively far apart, and a simple, long-distance connection is needed.

- **Types:**

    - **UART (Universal Asynchronous Receiver/Transmitter):** UART is a widely used serial communication protocol that allows devices to communicate asynchronously without a shared clock signal. It's common in applications like RS-232 and RS-485.

    - **SPI (Serial Peripheral Interface):** SPI is a synchronous serial communication protocol used for short-distance, high-speed communication between microcontrollers and peripheral devices like sensors and displays.

    - **I2C (Inter-Integrated Circuit):** I2C is a multi-master, multi-slave serial communication protocol often used for communication between ICs (integrated circuits), sensors, and other peripherals on a PCB.

2. Parallel Communication:

- **Definition:** Parallel communication involves sending multiple bits simultaneously over multiple wires (parallel lines). It's typically faster than serial communication but requires more wires and is suitable for short distances.

- **Types:**

    - **Parallel Ports:** These use multiple wires to send data and control signals between the CPU and external devices. Examples include the parallel printer port (Centronics) and parallel ATA (PATA) for hard drives and optical drives.

- **Parallel Buses:** These are used internally within a computer to connect components like the CPU, RAM, and peripherals. Examples include the system bus and memory bus.

3. USB (Universal Serial Bus):

- **Definition:** USB is a widely adopted standard for connecting a wide range of peripherals, such as keyboards, mice, printers, storage devices, cameras, and smartphones, to computers and other host devices.

- **Characteristics:**

  - USB offers a convenient and standardized way to connect devices and supports hot-plugging (connecting and disconnecting devices without turning off the computer).

  - USB can provide power to connected devices (USB-powered devices).

  - USB supports different data transfer rates (USB 2.0, USB 3.0, USB 3.1) to accommodate various device requirements.

  - USB also supports a variety of device classes, including Human Interface Devices (HID), Mass Storage, Audio, Video, and more.

4. Ethernet:

- **Definition:** Ethernet is a widely used networking technology for connecting devices within local area networks (LANs) and the internet.

- **Characteristics:**

  - Ethernet uses twisted-pair or fiber-optic cables to transmit data packets.

  - It supports various speeds, such as 10/100/1000 Mbps (Fast Ethernet, Gigabit Ethernet), and 10 Gbps and 100 Gbps for high-speed data center applications.

  - Ethernet relies on the Ethernet protocol suite, including Ethernet frames, TCP/IP, and UDP/IP for data transmission and network communication.

  - Ethernet is commonly used in scenarios like internet access, local network file sharing, and video streaming.

5. Wireless Communication:

- **Definition:** Wireless communication involves transmitting and receiving data without physical cables. Various wireless technologies exist for different purposes.

- **Types:**

  - **Wi-Fi (Wireless Fidelity):** Wi-Fi is a wireless LAN technology that allows devices to connect to the internet or local networks without physical cables.

  - **Bluetooth:** Bluetooth is used for short-range wireless connections between devices, such as wireless headphones, keyboards, and IoT devices.

  - **NFC (Near Field Communication):** NFC enables close-range communication (a few centimeters) between devices for tasks like contactless payments and data transfer.

- **Cellular Networks:** Mobile devices use cellular networks (e.g., 3G, 4G, 5G) for long-range wireless communication with the internet and other devices.

- **RFID (Radio-Frequency Identification):** RFID technology is used for tracking and identifying objects and products in various industries.

These I/O communication methods serve different purposes and are chosen based on factors like data transfer speed, distance, power requirements, device compatibility, and the specific application's needs. The choice of communication method plays a crucial role in determining the efficiency and functionality of a system or device.

- ## Disk I/O and RAID Systems

Disk I/O (Input/Output) and RAID (Redundant Array of Independent Disks) systems are crucial components of data storage and management in computer systems. They play a significant role in ensuring data integrity, availability, and performance. Let's explore both concepts in detail:

Disk I/O (Input/Output):

Disk I/O refers to the process of reading data from and writing data to storage devices, primarily hard disk drives (HDDs) and solid-state drives (SSDs). Disk I/O is a critical operation in computer systems because it involves transferring data between the CPU, memory, and storage devices. Understanding and optimizing disk I/O is essential for achieving efficient and responsive storage subsystems. Here are key aspects of disk I/O:

1. **Components of Disk I/O:**

   - **Read Operations:** Reading data from storage devices into memory is essential for retrieving files, running applications, and accessing databases.

   - **Write Operations:** Writing data from memory to storage devices is crucial for saving files, updating databases, and preserving system state.

   - **File Systems:** File systems, such as NTFS (Windows), ext4 (Linux), and APFS (macOS), manage the organization and access of data on storage devices.

   - **Caching:** Caching techniques, like read and write caching, improve I/O performance by storing frequently accessed data in memory for faster retrieval and writing.

2. **I/O Performance Factors:**

   - **Seek Time:** The time it takes for the disk's read/write head to move to the correct track (seek) is a significant factor in I/O performance for HDDs.

   - **Latency:** Disk latency includes seek time, rotational delay (for HDDs), and transfer time. Reducing latency is critical for improving I/O speed.

   - **Throughput:** Throughput measures the rate at which data can be read from or written to a storage device. It's crucial for bulk data transfer.

   - **Queue Depth:** Disk controllers and operating systems manage a queue of pending I/O requests. A higher queue depth can improve performance by optimizing I/O order.

3. **Optimizing Disk I/O:**

- **File System Optimization:** Choosing the right file system and optimizing its settings can significantly impact I/O performance.

- **I/O Scheduling Algorithms:** Operating systems use I/O schedulers to prioritize and optimize disk requests. Different algorithms can be used for various workloads.

- **RAID Systems:** RAID configurations (discussed below) can enhance both performance and data redundancy.

RAID Systems (Redundant Array of Independent Disks):

RAID is a technology that combines multiple physical drives into a single logical unit to improve data performance, fault tolerance, and redundancy. RAID arrays distribute data across drives in different ways, depending on the RAID level used. Here are some key aspects of RAID systems:

1. **RAID Levels:**

   - **RAID 0 (Striping):** Data is split into blocks and written across multiple drives simultaneously. RAID 0 improves performance but offers no redundancy.

   - **RAID 1 (Mirroring):** Data is duplicated on two or more drives, providing redundancy. RAID 1 offers fault tolerance but doesn't improve performance.

   - **RAID 5 (Striping with Parity):** Data is striped across multiple drives, and parity information is distributed across drives. RAID 5 offers a balance of performance and redundancy.

   - **RAID 6 (Double Parity):** Similar to RAID 5, but with two sets of parity data for enhanced fault tolerance.

   - **RAID 10 (1+0 or Mirrored Stripes):** Combines elements of RAID 1 and RAID 0. Data is mirrored, and the mirrors are striped. RAID 10 offers both performance and redundancy.

2. **RAID Controllers:** Hardware RAID controllers manage RAID configurations independently of the host CPU and provide dedicated processing power for RAID tasks. Software RAID is managed by the host CPU and relies on the operating system.

3. **Benefits of RAID:**

   - **Data Redundancy:** RAID configurations provide data redundancy, protecting against drive failures and data loss.

   - **Performance Improvement:** Some RAID levels (e.g., RAID 0, RAID 5) can significantly improve data access and transfer speeds.

   - **Increased Capacity:** RAID arrays can offer increased storage capacity by combining multiple drives into a single logical volume.

4. **RAID Considerations:**

   - **Cost:** Hardware RAID controllers and additional drives can be costly.

   - **Complexity:** Setting up and managing RAID configurations can be complex, especially for RAID levels involving parity (e.g., RAID 5, RAID 6).

- **Rebuild Time:** Rebuilding a RAID array after a drive failure can take time, and during this period, there is a risk of another drive failing.

In summary, disk I/O is the process of reading from and writing to storage devices, and it plays a critical role in computer system performance. RAID systems provide various ways to improve data redundancy and performance, depending on the specific requirements of a system. The choice of RAID level and optimization strategies should align with the intended use and goals of the storage subsystem.

Chapter 6: Pipeline and Superscalar Processors

- ### Instruction Pipelining Concepts

Instruction pipelining is a fundamental concept in computer architecture and microprocessor design that enables the concurrent execution of multiple instructions to improve processor throughput and overall performance. It breaks down the execution of instructions into multiple stages, with each stage responsible for a specific task. Here, I'll explain instruction pipelining in detail:

Basic Idea of Instruction Pipelining:

Instruction pipelining is inspired by assembly lines in manufacturing, where multiple tasks are performed in parallel to increase production efficiency. In the context of computer processors, it allows instructions to overlap their execution, effectively reducing the time it takes to complete a single instruction. The pipeline consists of several stages, and at each clock cycle, a new instruction is fetched while the previous instruction(s) progress through the pipeline.

Key Concepts in Instruction Pipelining:

1. **Pipeline Stages:** The pipeline is divided into several stages, each responsible for a specific task in the instruction execution process. The typical pipeline stages are:

   - **Fetch (IF):** Fetch the next instruction from memory.

   - **Decode (ID):** Decode the instruction and determine the required operands.

   - **Execute (EX):** Perform the actual operation, such as arithmetic or logical calculations.

   - **Memory (MEM):** Access memory (read or write) if needed.

   - **Write-back (WB):** Write the result back to registers.

2. **Instruction Throughput:** Pipelining allows for an instruction to be completed in multiple clock cycles, but it also enables a new instruction to enter the pipeline at each clock cycle. This results in an improvement in instruction throughput and overall system performance.

3. **Hazards:** Hazards are situations in pipelining that can slow down or stall the pipeline's progress. Three common types of hazards are:

   - **Structural Hazards:** These occur when multiple pipeline stages require the same hardware resource simultaneously, leading to contention. For example, both the memory and execution stages requiring access to the memory subsystem simultaneously.

- **Data Hazards:** Data hazards occur when a later instruction depends on the result of a previous instruction that has not yet completed. This can lead to stalls or incorrect results.

- **Control Hazards:** Control hazards arise when there is uncertainty about the next instruction to be executed. Branch instructions can cause control hazards if the branch target is not yet known.

4. **Forwarding:** Forwarding (also known as data forwarding or data hazard detection) is a technique used to mitigate data hazards. It involves sending data directly from one pipeline stage to another, bypassing intermediate stages, to resolve data dependencies quickly.

5. **Branch Prediction:** Branch instructions can cause control hazards by introducing uncertainty into the pipeline. Branch prediction techniques, such as branch target prediction and branch outcome prediction, are used to reduce the impact of branch instructions on pipeline performance.

6. **Pipeline Flush:** In cases where a hazard cannot be resolved, the pipeline may need to be flushed. This means discarding all instructions in the pipeline after the instruction causing the hazard and starting over. Pipeline flushing can have a significant impact on performance.

Advantages of Instruction Pipelining:

1. **Increased Throughput:** Pipelining allows for multiple instructions to be in different stages of execution simultaneously, improving instruction throughput.

2. **Better Resource Utilization:** Multiple stages can operate concurrently, ensuring that processor resources (e.g., ALUs, memory units) are used efficiently.

3. **Reduced Execution Time:** Instructions can be completed in less time due to parallelism, resulting in faster program execution.

Challenges and Limitations:

1. **Complexity:** Pipelined processors are more complex to design and manage compared to non-pipelined processors.

2. **Hazards:** Handling hazards (structural, data, and control hazards) can be challenging and may require additional logic to resolve.

3. **Increased Latency:** While pipelining reduces the execution time of individual instructions, it can introduce additional latency due to pipeline stages and hazards.

In summary, instruction pipelining is a powerful technique used in modern microprocessor design to improve processor throughput and performance by breaking down the execution of instructions into multiple stages that can operate concurrently. However, it also introduces challenges related to hazards and pipeline management, which must be addressed to maximize its benefits.

- ## Hazards and Pipeline Stalls

Hazards and pipeline stalls are important concepts in computer architecture, especially when dealing with pipelined processors. Pipelining is a technique used to enhance the performance of CPUs by breaking down instruction execution into multiple stages. However, hazards can arise when instructions in a pipeline interfere with each other, leading to stalls or delays in the pipeline's operation. Let's explore hazards and pipeline stalls in detail:

1. Structural Hazards:

- **Definition:** Structural hazards occur when there is a conflict over the use of specific hardware resources within the CPU.

- **Example:** In a simple pipeline, if one instruction is trying to access memory (e.g., a load operation) while another instruction is attempting to write to memory (e.g., a store operation), a structural hazard arises. This conflict can lead to a stall in the pipeline because the memory unit cannot be accessed by both instructions simultaneously.

2. Data Hazards:

- **Definition:** Data hazards, also known as data dependencies, arise when there is a dependency between the data used by one instruction and the data produced by another instruction in the pipeline.

- **Types of Data Hazards:**

  - **Read-after-Write (RAW) Hazard:** Occurs when an instruction depends on the result of a previous instruction.

  - **Write-after-Read (WAR) Hazard:** Occurs when a previous instruction depends on the result of a subsequent instruction.

  - **Write-after-Write (WAW) Hazard:** Occurs when two instructions both attempt to write to the same register or memory location.

- **Example (RAW Hazard):**

markdownCopy code

1. ADD R1, R2, R3 (R1 = R2 + R3) 2. SUB R4, R1, R5 (R4 = R1 - R5)

In this case, the second instruction depends on the result of the first instruction (R1), resulting in a RAW hazard. The pipeline may stall until the first instruction completes its execution.

3. Control Hazards:

- **Definition:** Control hazards, also known as branch hazards, occur when the pipeline encounters a branch instruction, and the outcome of the branch is uncertain. This can lead to a stall in the pipeline.

- **Example:** Consider a branch instruction with a condition, and the pipeline has already fetched and partially executed instructions following the branch. If the branch outcome is determined late in the pipeline, there may be a need to flush or discard the incorrect instructions and fetch the correct ones, leading to a pipeline stall.

Pipeline stalls can be mitigated using various techniques:

1. Forwarding (Data Hazard Resolution):

- Forwarding, also known as data forwarding or bypassing, involves sending data directly from the execution stage to the stages that need it, bypassing the register file. This helps resolve data hazards without stalls.

2. Branch Prediction (Control Hazard Resolution):

- Branch prediction techniques, such as branch target buffers (BTB) and speculative execution, can be used to predict the outcome of branch instructions, reducing control hazards.

3. Compiler Optimizations:

- Compiler optimizations, like instruction scheduling and loop unrolling, can help reduce data hazards by reordering instructions to minimize dependencies.

In conclusion, hazards in a pipelined processor can lead to pipeline stalls, reducing CPU efficiency. Structural, data, and control hazards are common types of hazards that can occur. Techniques like forwarding, branch prediction, and compiler optimizations are used to mitigate these hazards and improve pipeline performance.

- ## Superscalar Architecture and Multiple Issue Processors

Superscalar architecture and multiple issue processors are advanced computer processor designs aimed at achieving higher levels of instruction-level parallelism (ILP) and improving the overall performance of a computer system. These concepts are primarily used in modern high-performance microprocessors. Let's delve into each of these concepts in detail:

1. Superscalar Architecture:

Superscalar architecture is a type of CPU design that allows the processor to execute multiple instructions in parallel during a single clock cycle. This design concept is based on the idea of exploiting ILP by issuing and executing multiple instructions simultaneously. Here are some key features and components of a superscalar architecture:

- **Instruction Fetch:** The processor fetches multiple instructions per cycle from the instruction cache or memory.

- **Instruction Decode:** The fetched instructions are then decoded to identify their types, dependencies, and execution units required.

- **Issue Logic:** In superscalar processors, there is issue logic that determines which instructions can be executed concurrently without violating data dependencies.

- **Execution Units:** Superscalar processors have multiple execution units for various types of instructions, such as integer, floating-point, load/store, etc.

- **Out-of-Order Execution**: Instructions are often executed out of order if their data dependencies allow. This helps in maximizing processor utilization.

- **Register Renaming:** To eliminate data hazards, superscalar processors use register renaming techniques, which allow multiple instructions to use the same architectural registers without conflicts.

- **Reorder Buffer:** A reorder buffer is used to keep track of the execution order of instructions and to commit the results in the correct order to maintain program correctness.

- **Dynamic Scheduling**: Dynamic scheduling mechanisms decide at runtime which instructions to issue and execute, considering data availability and resource availability.

Superscalar processors are highly complex and require sophisticated hardware and control mechanisms to ensure efficient execution. They excel at executing a mix of instructions with varying dependencies and types simultaneously, which can significantly boost performance for applications with high ILP.

2. Multiple Issue Processors:

Multiple issue processors are a subclass of superscalar processors that can dispatch and execute more than one instruction per clock cycle, even if those instructions are not fully independent. They take advantage of ILP by issuing multiple instructions from a single instruction stream (program) in a single clock cycle. Here are some important aspects of multiple issue processors:

- **Issue Width**: The issue width refers to the number of instructions that can be issued simultaneously in a single clock cycle. For example, a processor with a 4-issue width can dispatch and execute four instructions in parallel during one clock cycle.

- **Dependencies Handling**: Multiple issue processors use advanced dependency checking and forwarding mechanisms to identify and resolve dependencies between instructions. They often employ techniques like scoreboarding and reservation stations.

- **Compiler Support**: To fully utilize a multiple issue processor, compilers play a crucial role in scheduling and organizing instructions to minimize dependencies and maximize parallelism.

- **Performance Gains**: Multiple issue processors can provide substantial performance gains for applications that have a high level of ILP. However, their effectiveness may vary depending on the specific workload and how well the compiler can exploit parallelism.

Multiple issue processors are typically found in high-performance CPUs designed for tasks like scientific computing, multimedia processing, and gaming, where the workload can benefit significantly from parallel execution.

In summary, superscalar architecture and multiple issue processors are advanced CPU designs that aim to execute multiple instructions simultaneously to improve performance by exploiting ILP. While they offer substantial performance benefits, they also require complex hardware and compiler support to achieve their full potential.

- Out-of-Order Execution and Speculative Execution

Out-of-order execution and speculative execution are advanced techniques employed in modern computer processors to enhance their performance by optimizing the execution of instructions. These techniques allow processors to execute instructions in a more efficient and parallel manner. Let's delve into each of these concepts in detail:

1. Out-of-Order Execution:

Out-of-order execution (OoOE) is a CPU design technique that allows instructions to be executed in a sequence different from the order in which they appear in the program. The primary goal of OoOE is to improve instruction-level parallelism (ILP) and make better use of the available execution resources. Here's how it works:

- **Instruction Issue:** When instructions are fetched and decoded, they are placed in a queue known as the instruction window or reorder buffer, which preserves their original program order.

- **Dependency Checking:** The processor checks for data dependencies among instructions. Instructions with unresolved dependencies cannot proceed until the required data becomes available.

- **Out-of-Order Execution:** If an instruction has no unresolved dependencies and the required execution unit is available, it can be executed out of order, potentially ahead of instructions that appear earlier in the program.

- **Commit Stage:** After execution, instructions are re-ordered in their original program order in the commit stage. This ensures that the architectural state of the CPU remains consistent with the program's intended order of execution.

- **Benefits:** OoOE allows the processor to keep execution units busy by executing independent instructions in parallel. It helps mitigate stalls caused by data dependencies and improves overall throughput and performance.

- **Drawbacks:** OoOE processors are more complex and require additional hardware resources for dependency tracking and re-ordering. They can also introduce challenges in maintaining precise exceptions and debugging.

Out-of-order execution and speculative execution are advanced techniques employed in modern computer processors to enhance their performance by optimizing the execution of instructions. These techniques allow processors to execute instructions in a more efficient and parallel manner. Let's delve into each of these concepts in detail:

2. Speculative Execution:

Speculative execution is a CPU optimization technique that involves executing instructions before it is certain they are needed, with the assumption that they will likely be needed based on branch prediction. The goal of speculative execution is to reduce the impact of branch mispredictions and improve overall performance. Here's how it works:

- **Branch Prediction**: Speculative execution relies on branch prediction to anticipate the outcome of conditional branches. Predictions are made based on historical behavior and patterns in the code.

- **Speculative Instruction Execution:** The processor speculatively executes instructions along the predicted path, even before the branch condition is fully evaluated. This means instructions are executed speculatively, assuming that the branch prediction is correct.

- **Rollback:** If the branch prediction is incorrect (i.e., a branch misprediction occurs), the speculatively executed instructions are discarded, and the correct path is taken. This process is known as rollback.

- **Benefits**: Speculative execution can significantly reduce the performance penalty associated with branch mispredictions, as it keeps the processor busy with useful work while waiting for the branch resolution.

- **Drawbacks**: Speculative execution introduces complexity and can have security implications. In some cases, it can potentially leak sensitive information through side-channel attacks, such as Spectre and Meltdown vulnerabilities.

Both out-of-order execution and speculative execution are essential techniques in modern high-performance processors. They work together to extract maximum parallelism from code, minimize execution stalls, and improve overall CPU performance. However, they also require careful design and security considerations to address potential challenges and vulnerabilities.

Chapter 7: Parallel and Vector Processing

- Flynn's Taxonomy: SISD, SIMD, MISD, MIMD

Flynn's Taxonomy is a classification system for parallel processing architectures, categorizing them based on the number of instruction streams (I) and data streams (D) they can handle simultaneously. It was proposed by Michael J. Flynn in 1966 and has been a foundational concept in the field of computer architecture. Here, I'll provide detailed explanations of each category within Flynn's Taxonomy:

1. SISD - Single Instruction, Single Data:

Explanation: In an SISD architecture, there is a single processor that executes a single instruction stream and operates on a single data stream at a time. This is essentially the traditional von Neumann architecture where instructions are fetched one at a time from memory and processed sequentially.

Characteristics:

- Sequential execution of instructions.
- Well-suited for single-threaded tasks and non-parallelizable workloads.
- Limited in terms of processing power and throughput for parallel tasks.

2. SIMD - Single Instruction, Multiple Data:

Explanation: In a SIMD architecture, there are multiple processing units (e.g., CPU cores or specialized SIMD units) that execute the same instruction on multiple data elements simultaneously. This allows for parallel processing of data in a highly coordinated manner.

Characteristics:

- All processing units execute the same instruction in lockstep.
- Ideal for tasks that can be parallelized, such as vector and matrix operations, graphics processing, and certain scientific simulations.
- Requires data-level parallelism, where the same operation is applied to multiple data elements.

3. MISD - Multiple Instruction, Single Data:

Explanation: MISD architectures are relatively rare and less commonly encountered in practice. In an MISD system, multiple processing units execute different instructions on the same data stream.

Characteristics:

- Each processing unit applies a distinct operation to the same data stream.
- Typically used in highly specialized scenarios, such as fault-tolerant systems or parallel computing research.

4. MIMD - Multiple Instruction, Multiple Data:

Explanation: MIMD architectures are the most versatile and common type of parallel processing. In a MIMD system, multiple processing units each have their own instruction stream and data stream, allowing them to work independently on different tasks or data sets.

Characteristics:

- Each processing unit operates independently and can execute different instructions on separate data.
- Ideal for general-purpose parallel computing tasks, such as scientific simulations, multi-core processors, clusters, and distributed computing.
- Offers the highest degree of parallelism and flexibility.

Each of these categories has its own set of advantages and limitations. The choice of architecture depends on the specific requirements of the application, the nature of the data, and the available hardware. Modern computers and computing clusters often utilize MIMD architectures due to their flexibility and ability to handle a wide range of parallel workloads. SIMD architectures are commonly found in specialized processors like GPUs, where data-level parallelism is critical for tasks such as rendering and machine learning.

- ## Parallel Processing Architectures

Parallel processing architectures are computer systems designed to perform multiple tasks or process data simultaneously. These architectures are particularly valuable in tasks that require high computational power and speed, such as scientific simulations, data analysis, and artificial intelligence. Here, I'll provide an in-depth overview of parallel processing architectures.

1. Flynn's Taxonomy:

Flynn's Taxonomy categorizes parallel processing architectures based on the number of instruction streams (I) and data streams (D) they can handle simultaneously. There are four categories:

- **Single Instruction, Single Data (SISD):** Conventional serial computing, where a single CPU executes a single instruction on a single piece of data at a time.

- **Single Instruction, Multiple Data (SIMD):** Multiple processing units execute the same instruction on different data elements in parallel. This architecture is commonly used in applications like graphics processing and scientific simulations.
- **Multiple Instruction, Single Data (MISD):** Multiple processing units execute different instructions on the same data stream, which is a less common configuration.
- **Multiple Instruction, Multiple Data (MIMD):** Multiple processing units execute different instructions on separate data streams. This is the most versatile and common parallel processing architecture found in multi-core CPUs and distributed computing clusters.

2. Parallel Processing Architectures in MIMD:

- **Shared Memory Systems**: In these systems, multiple processors share a single, global memory space. They communicate and synchronize through this shared memory. Common examples include multi-core CPUs and symmetric multiprocessing (SMP) systems.
- **Distributed Memory Systems**: In this architecture, processors have their own local memory and communicate through message-passing protocols. Examples include clusters of computers, where each node has its own memory.
- **NUMA (Non-Uniform Memory Access) Systems:** NUMA is a variation of shared memory architecture in which memory access times can vary depending on the processor's proximity to the memory module. This is common in large-scale servers.
- **Multithreading:** Multithreaded processors execute multiple threads simultaneously. This can be done at the instruction level (fine-grained) or at a higher level where entire threads are scheduled.
- **GPU (Graphics Processing Unit):** Originally designed for graphics rendering, modern GPUs have evolved into massively parallel processors capable of handling a wide range of general-purpose tasks through APIs like CUDA and OpenCL.
- **Cluster and Grid Computing:** Combining multiple computers or servers into a cluster or grid to work in parallel on a task. These systems often use distributed memory architectures.

3. Parallel Programming Models:

- **Shared Memory Parallelism**: Programming models like OpenMP and Pthreads are used to create parallel programs for shared memory systems.
- **Message Passing**: In distributed memory systems, programs communicate by passing messages between processes. MPI (Message Passing Interface) is a widely used standard for this purpose.
- **Data Parallelism:** In SIMD architectures, data parallelism is used, where the same operation is performed on multiple data elements simultaneously.
- **Task Parallelism:** In MIMD architectures, task parallelism involves breaking a problem into smaller tasks that can be executed in parallel. This is often used in multithreading.

4. Challenges in Parallel Processing:

- **Data Dependencies**: Managing data dependencies and ensuring proper synchronization between parallel tasks.

- **Load Balancing**: Distributing work evenly among processors to avoid bottlenecks.
- **Communication Overhead**: Minimizing the time spent on inter-process communication.
- **Scalability**: Ensuring that the architecture can effectively scale with an increasing number of processors.
- **Fault Tolerance**: Designing systems that can continue functioning in the presence of hardware failures.

Parallel processing architectures have become essential in today's computing landscape, enabling faster and more efficient processing of complex tasks. However, effectively utilizing parallelism requires careful consideration of the architecture, programming models, and the specific demands of the application.

- ## SIMD and Vector Processors

SIMD (Single Instruction, Multiple Data) and vector processors are both types of architectures designed to perform parallel processing on multiple data elements simultaneously. They are particularly well-suited for tasks that involve large datasets and repetitive operations. Here, I'll provide detailed explanations of SIMD and vector processors:

SIMD (Single Instruction, Multiple Data):

SIMD is a parallel processing architecture in which a single instruction is applied to multiple data elements in parallel. In other words, all processing units execute the same instruction at the same time, but on different data elements. Here are some key features and characteristics of SIMD architectures:

1. **Parallelism**: SIMD architectures are highly parallel because they perform the same operation on multiple data elements concurrently. This is well-suited for tasks with inherent data-level parallelism, such as array operations and multimedia processing.

2. **Instructions**: SIMD processors have a special set of instructions that enable the same operation to be applied to multiple data elements in a single instruction. These instructions are typically vectorized, meaning they work on vector registers.

3. **Vector Registers**: SIMD processors use vector registers to store and manipulate data elements. Vector registers can hold multiple data values, such as floating-point numbers or integers, and the SIMD instructions operate on these registers.

4. **Applications**:

   - **Graphics Processing**: SIMD is widely used in GPUs (Graphics Processing Units) to accelerate tasks like rendering, image processing, and video decoding.

   - **Scientific Computing**: SIMD instructions are valuable for scientific simulations, where large datasets are processed in parallel.

   - **Multimedia**: Audio and video codecs often employ SIMD to process data streams efficiently.

5. **Examples**:

- Intel SSE (Streaming SIMD Extensions)

- ARM NEON

- AMD XOP (eXtended Operations)

- NVIDIA CUDA (for GPU programming)

Vector Processors:

Vector processors are a type of SIMD architecture designed specifically for vector operations. They excel at performing the same operation on a large set of data elements organized in vectors. Here are some key features and characteristics of vector processors:

1. **Vector Operations**: Vector processors are optimized for vector operations, where a single instruction operates on entire vectors of data simultaneously. A vector is a one-dimensional array of data elements.

2. **Vector Length**: The size of the vector, often referred to as the "vector length" or "stride," determines how many data elements are processed in parallel. Vector processors can have varying vector lengths to accommodate different types of tasks.

3. **Memory Bandwidth**: Vector processors typically require high memory bandwidth to keep the vector registers supplied with data. This is because they can consume data at a high rate due to parallelism.

4. **Applications**:

    - **Scientific and Engineering Simulations**: Vector processors are well-suited for numerical simulations and simulations in fields like physics and engineering.

    - **Supercomputing**: Many supercomputers employ vector processors for high-performance computing tasks.

5. **Examples**:

    - Cray vector processors (e.g., Cray-1, Cray-2)

    - Fujitsu vector processors (e.g., Fujitsu VP)

    - NEC SX series

Vector processors were more prevalent in the past, particularly in supercomputers, but their use has become less common with the rise of more general-purpose processors and GPUs. Nonetheless, they remain crucial for certain scientific and high-performance computing applications that heavily rely on vectorized computations.

In summary, SIMD architectures, including vector processors, are designed to leverage parallelism by executing the same instruction on multiple data elements simultaneously. SIMD is widely used in various computing domains to accelerate data-intensive and parallelizable tasks.

- ## Multicore Processors and Parallel Programming

Multicore processors and parallel programming are closely related topics, as multicore processors are designed to execute multiple tasks or threads in parallel. In this detailed explanation, I'll delve into both multicore processors and the concepts of parallel programming:

Multicore Processors:

A multicore processor is a type of microprocessor that integrates multiple CPU cores onto a single chip. Each core is essentially a separate processing unit capable of executing instructions independently. Here are key aspects of multicore processors:

1. **Core Count**: Multicore processors can have varying numbers of CPU cores, typically ranging from two cores (dual-core) to many cores (such as octa-core or more). The core count depends on the specific processor design and intended use.

2. **Parallelism**: The primary advantage of multicore processors is their ability to perform parallel processing. Tasks can be divided among the available cores, and each core can execute its own set of instructions simultaneously.

3. **Improved Performance**: Multicore processors can deliver significantly improved performance for multi-threaded and parallelizable workloads. They can execute multiple tasks concurrently, making them well-suited for multitasking and computationally intensive applications.

4. **Types of Multicore Processors**:

   - **Symmetric Multiprocessing (SMP)**: In SMP systems, all CPU cores are generally identical and have equal access to the system's memory and resources. This architecture is commonly found in desktop and server CPUs.

   - **Asymmetric Multiprocessing (AMP)**: AMP systems may have cores with different capabilities. Some cores may be optimized for high-performance tasks, while others are energy-efficient for less demanding workloads. This approach is often seen in mobile processors.

5. **Cache Sharing**: Multicore processors typically share various levels of cache memory between cores. Effective cache management is crucial for optimizing performance in multicore systems.

6. **Programming Considerations**: To fully leverage multicore processors, software must be designed or adapted to use multiple threads or processes in parallel.

Parallel Programming:

Parallel programming is a programming paradigm that focuses on breaking down a task into smaller subtasks that can be executed concurrently, either on multiple CPU cores within a multicore processor or across multiple processors or nodes in a distributed system. Here are important aspects of parallel programming:

1. **Parallelism Models**:

   - **Task Parallelism**: In task parallelism, different threads or processes work on different tasks simultaneously. This approach is suitable for applications where tasks can be executed independently.

- **Data Parallelism**: Data parallelism involves performing the same operation on multiple data elements in parallel. It is often used in applications like scientific simulations and multimedia processing.

2. **Concurrency Control**:

   - **Synchronization**: To avoid data conflicts and ensure proper coordination, synchronization mechanisms like locks, semaphores, and barriers are used.

   - **Race Conditions**: Developers must be aware of race conditions, where multiple threads or processes attempt to access shared data simultaneously, potentially leading to unpredictable behavior.

3. **Parallel Programming Models and Libraries**:

   - **OpenMP**: A popular API for shared memory parallel programming that simplifies adding parallelism to C, C++, and Fortran code.

   - **MPI (Message Passing Interface)**: A widely used library for message-passing parallel programming in distributed memory systems.

   - **CUDA and OpenCL**: APIs for parallel programming on GPUs, enabling high-performance computing and general-purpose GPU (GPGPU) computing.

4. **Load Balancing**: Ensuring that work is evenly distributed among threads or processes is crucial for maximizing parallel processing performance.

5. **Scalability**: Parallel programs should be designed with scalability in mind to accommodate varying numbers of CPU cores or processors efficiently.

6. **Debugging and Profiling**: Debugging parallel programs can be challenging due to issues like race conditions and deadlocks. Profiling tools help identify performance bottlenecks and optimize parallel code.

Parallel programming is essential for harnessing the power of multicore processors and distributed computing environments. It allows applications to take advantage of the increasing number of cores in modern CPUs, leading to faster and more efficient execution of tasks. However, it also introduces challenges related to concurrency management and ensuring correct program behavior in parallel execution.

Chapter 8: Instruction-Level Parallelism

- ## Dynamic Scheduling and Tomasulo Algorithm

Dynamic scheduling and the Tomasulo algorithm are techniques used in modern computer architectures to improve instruction-level parallelism (ILP) and enhance the execution of instructions in a processor's execution units. Here, I'll provide detailed explanations of both concepts:

Dynamic Scheduling:

Dynamic scheduling is a technique used in superscalar and out-of-order execution processors to execute instructions in an order that maximizes the utilization of execution units and minimizes idle time. It differs from static scheduling, where instructions are scheduled in the order they appear in the program.

Here's how dynamic scheduling works:

1. **Instruction Issue:** Instructions are fetched from memory and decoded. The processor checks if the operands required for an instruction are available in the registers or memory.

2. **Scheduling:** Instructions are scheduled for execution based on the availability of execution units and operands. The goal is to minimize dependencies between instructions and maximize parallel execution.

3. **Out-of-Order Execution:** In dynamic scheduling, instructions can be executed out of order, meaning an instruction with no data dependencies can be executed ahead of dependent instructions, as long as the required resources are available.

4. **Reservation Stations:** To facilitate dynamic scheduling, processors often use structures called reservation stations. These are buffers that hold instructions and their operands until they are ready for execution. Each execution unit typically has its reservation station.

5. **Register Renaming:** Dynamic scheduling also involves register renaming, which allows multiple instructions to use the same architectural register names while maintaining separate physical registers. This avoids data hazards and simplifies out-of-order execution.

6. **Reordering Buffer:** To ensure that instructions are committed in program order, processors maintain a reordering buffer. Instructions are dispatched to execution units from the reservation stations and retire (commit) in program order.

Dynamic scheduling enables processors to exploit instruction-level parallelism by allowing independent instructions to execute concurrently. It helps mitigate issues like data hazards and instruction dependencies, resulting in more efficient CPU execution.

Tomasulo Algorithm:

The Tomasulo algorithm is a specific dynamic scheduling algorithm used to implement out-of-order execution in modern processors. It was developed by Robert Tomasulo at IBM in the 1960s and has since become a fundamental concept in computer architecture. Here's how the Tomasulo algorithm works:

1. **Reservation Stations:** In the Tomasulo algorithm, instructions are dispatched to reservation stations associated with functional units (e.g., ALUs, FPUs). Each reservation station holds the instruction and its operands until they are available.

2. **Issue Stage:** During this stage, instructions are issued to the functional units if their operands are ready. If an operand is not ready, the instruction waits in the reservation station.

3. **Execution Stage:** Once all operands are available, an instruction begins executing in its associated functional unit. If multiple instructions are waiting for the same functional unit, they are scheduled in a first-come, first-served order.

4. **Write-Back Stage:** When an instruction completes its execution, the result is broadcasted to all reservation stations that are waiting for that result. This enables dependent instructions to proceed.

5. **Commit Stage:** Instructions are committed (retired) in program order from the reordering buffer. This ensures that instructions are completed and written to architectural registers in the correct sequence, even though they may execute out of order.

The Tomasulo algorithm's key advantage is its ability to handle data hazards and out-of-order execution efficiently. By using reservation stations, it can identify and resolve data dependencies dynamically, allowing instructions with no dependencies to execute concurrently and maximizing processor throughput.

Modern processors, including many CPUs and GPUs, use variations of the Tomasulo algorithm or similar techniques to achieve high levels of instruction-level parallelism, making them capable of executing multiple instructions simultaneously and improving overall performance.

- ## Branch Prediction and Speculative Execution

Branch prediction and speculative execution are advanced techniques employed in modern computer architectures to enhance the performance of processors by mitigating the impact of conditional branches and improving instruction throughput. Here's a detailed explanation of each concept:

Branch Prediction:

In computer programs, conditional branches (e.g., if statements and loops) introduce a decision point where the program can follow one of multiple paths based on a condition. Predicting the outcome of these branches accurately is crucial for maintaining a high instruction throughput in processors. Branch prediction aims to predict which path a conditional branch will take before the outcome is known. It allows the processor to start fetching and executing instructions along the predicted path, rather than waiting for the actual branch resolution.

Key components and considerations of branch prediction:

1. **Branch Instruction**: A branch instruction is one that can change the program's control flow based on a condition, such as a comparison between values.

2. **Branch Target Address**: The predicted target address is the address of the instruction that the processor expects to execute next based on the branch prediction.

3. **Branch History Table (BHT)**: The BHT is a data structure that keeps track of past branch outcomes. It can be a simple two-bit saturating counter or a more complex data structure like a tournament predictor.

4. **Predictor Algorithms**: Various algorithms are used in branch prediction. Common approaches include static prediction, dynamic prediction (using history-based predictors), and tournament predictors that combine multiple predictors to improve accuracy.

5. **Mispredictions**: A misprediction occurs when the branch prediction is incorrect. When this happens, the processor must discard the speculative execution results and start executing from the correct branch target, incurring a performance penalty.

Speculative Execution:

Speculative execution is a technique that allows a processor to execute instructions ahead of the branch point (conditional branch) based on a predicted branch outcome. The processor speculatively executes instructions along the predicted path, assuming that the branch will resolve as predicted. Speculative execution aims to minimize the performance penalty associated with mispredicted branches by keeping the processor pipeline full and avoiding stalls.

Key components and considerations of speculative execution:

1. **Instruction Pipeline**: Modern processors use a pipeline architecture, where multiple instructions are in various stages of execution simultaneously. Speculative execution can fill the pipeline with instructions based on branch predictions.

2. **Rollback**: If a misprediction occurs, the processor must roll back or discard the speculative execution results. This involves flushing the instructions in the pipeline beyond the mispredicted branch and resuming execution from the correct path.

3. **Data Forwarding**: To prevent hazards related to data dependencies, speculative execution often involves data forwarding mechanisms to ensure that instructions have access to the correct data, even if it was modified speculatively.

4. **Performance Benefit**: Speculative execution can significantly improve the processor's throughput, especially in scenarios where branches are frequent and mispredictions are costly.

5. **Complexity**: Implementing speculative execution is complex, as it requires careful handling of mispredictions, data consistency, and rollback mechanisms. However, the performance benefits can outweigh the added complexity.

Speculative execution and branch prediction are integral to modern processor designs, allowing them to maintain high instruction throughput by effectively handling conditional branches. They are fundamental techniques for achieving the instruction-level parallelism that enables faster and more efficient execution of programs.

- ## Superscalar Processors and VLIW Architecture

Superscalar processors and Very Long Instruction Word (VLIW) architectures are two advanced CPU design approaches aimed at achieving high levels of instruction-level parallelism (ILP) to improve overall performance. Here's a detailed explanation of each concept:

Superscalar Processors:

Superscalar processors are a type of microprocessor that can execute multiple instructions simultaneously in a single clock cycle. Unlike scalar processors, which execute one instruction per clock cycle, superscalar processors fetch, decode, and execute multiple instructions simultaneously by exploiting ILP. Here's how they work:

1. **Multiple Execution Units:** Superscalar processors have multiple execution units, such as arithmetic logic units (ALUs) and floating-point units (FPUs), capable of performing different types of operations.

2. **Instruction Fetch and Decode:** Instructions are fetched from memory and decoded to identify their operation, source operands, and destination registers.

3. **Instruction Dispatch:** The processor dispatches instructions to available execution units based on their availability and dependencies. Dependencies between instructions are tracked to ensure correct execution.

4. **Parallel Execution:** Instructions that are independent of each other can be executed concurrently in different execution units. This allows multiple instructions to be processed simultaneously in a single clock cycle.

5. **Out-of-Order Execution:** Superscalar processors often employ out-of-order execution, meaning instructions can be executed out of the original program order as long as dependencies are satisfied. This minimizes idle time and maximizes instruction throughput.

6. **Register Renaming:** To prevent data hazards and ensure correct execution, superscalar processors use register renaming. This technique allows multiple instructions to use the same architectural register names while maintaining separate physical registers.

7. **Reordering Buffer:** A reordering buffer is used to track the original program order of instructions and ensure that they are committed in order, even though they may execute out of order.

8. **Dynamic Scheduling:** Superscalar processors often employ dynamic scheduling techniques, such as the Tomasulo algorithm, to manage execution and handle data dependencies efficiently.

Superscalar processors are widely used in modern CPUs, ranging from desktop and laptop processors to server-grade processors. They offer high performance and are capable of executing multiple instructions simultaneously, making them well-suited for applications with substantial ILP.

VLIW (Very Long Instruction Word) Architecture:

VLIW architecture is a CPU design approach that emphasizes compiler-generated parallelism rather than hardware-based dynamic scheduling. VLIW processors fetch and execute multiple instructions in parallel, but the compiler is responsible for scheduling these instructions at compile-time, rather than relying on complex hardware for out-of-order execution. Here's how VLIW architecture works:

1. **Static Scheduling:** In VLIW processors, the compiler determines the execution order of instructions during the compilation phase. It schedules instructions in a way that maximizes parallelism while adhering to dependencies and resource constraints.

2. **Instruction Bundles:** Instructions in a VLIW architecture are typically grouped into bundles or packets, each containing multiple instructions to be executed simultaneously in a single clock cycle.

3. **Compiler Assistance:** The VLIW architecture relies on a sophisticated compiler that performs instruction scheduling, register allocation, and dependency analysis to generate optimized code. The compiler's role is crucial in achieving efficient parallel execution.

4. **No Dynamic Scheduling Hardware:** Unlike superscalar processors, VLIW architectures do not require complex hardware for dynamic scheduling, speculative execution, or out-of-order execution. This simplifies the processor's microarchitecture.

5. **Explicit Parallelism:** VLIW architectures expose explicit parallelism to the compiler, which means the compiler must find and exploit parallelism within the code. If the compiler cannot

identify sufficient parallelism, the VLIW processor may not achieve its full performance potential.

6. **Code Compatibility:** Software compiled for VLIW processors is often specific to the target processor architecture, making it less portable than software for traditional CPUs.

VLIW architectures are commonly found in embedded systems and digital signal processors (DSPs) where code is highly optimized for specific applications. The effectiveness of VLIW architectures depends on the compiler's ability to extract parallelism from the code, and they are less flexible than superscalar processors in handling diverse workloads.

- ## Compiler Optimizations for ILP

Compiler optimizations for Instruction-Level Parallelism (ILP) play a crucial role in improving the performance of programs running on modern processors. These optimizations aim to restructure and optimize the code to enable the processor to execute multiple instructions in parallel. Here are some key compiler optimizations for ILP, explained in detail:

1. Loop Unrolling:

Explanation: Loop unrolling involves expanding loops by duplicating loop bodies or parts of them. This exposes more opportunities for instruction-level parallelism by allowing multiple iterations of the loop to execute simultaneously.

Benefits: It reduces the overhead of loop control and allows the compiler to schedule instructions from different iterations concurrently.

Example: Given a loop that adds elements of an array, unrolling it might involve processing two elements per iteration instead of one.

2. Loop Fusion and Fission:

Explanation: Loop fusion combines multiple loops into a single loop, reducing loop overhead. Loop fission splits a single loop into multiple smaller loops, which can be scheduled independently.

Benefits: Fusion reduces loop overhead, while fission can improve parallelism by allowing smaller loops to be scheduled independently.

Example: Combining loops that perform data initialization and computation into a single loop can reduce loop overhead.

3. Software Pipelining:

Explanation: Software pipelining is a technique that overlaps loop iterations by scheduling instructions from different iterations in a pipeline fashion. It maximizes instruction-level parallelism within loops.

Benefits: It keeps the execution units busy by issuing instructions from different iterations simultaneously.

Example: In a loop that performs matrix multiplication, software pipelining schedules the multiplications, additions, and updates in a way that minimizes pipeline stalls.

4. Instruction Scheduling:

Explanation: Instruction scheduling reorders instructions to minimize data dependencies and maximize parallel execution. This may involve out-of-order execution or rearranging instructions to fill execution units.

Benefits: Reduces pipeline stalls and ensures that instructions are executed as soon as their operands are available.

Example: Reordering instructions to execute independent calculations concurrently.

5. Dependency Analysis:

Explanation: Compiler optimizations analyze data dependencies between instructions to identify opportunities for parallelism. Common techniques include data flow analysis and use-def chains.

Benefits: Detecting dependencies allows the compiler to reorder instructions to exploit ILP without violating correctness.

Example: Detecting that an instruction's output is not used by subsequent instructions allows for parallel execution.

6. Auto-Vectorization:

Explanation: Auto-vectorization transforms scalar code into vectorized code by identifying and converting loops with regular data access patterns into vector operations.

Benefits: It utilizes vector execution units, like SIMD instructions, to process multiple data elements in parallel.

Example: A loop that adds two arrays element-wise can be auto-vectorized to perform the additions using vector instructions.

7. Register Allocation and Register Renaming:

Explanation: Efficient management of registers helps reduce data dependencies and enhances parallelism. Register renaming allows the compiler to use the same register name for multiple independent variables.

Benefits: Minimizes stalls due to register contention and enables the use of available registers optimally.

Example: Reusing registers for different variables in nested loops to reduce register pressure.

8. Instruction Reordering for Out-of-Order Execution:

Explanation: When targeting out-of-order execution processors, compilers can reorder instructions to maximize execution unit utilization.

Benefits: Exploits the processor's ability to execute instructions out of program order.

Example: Reordering independent instructions to fill execution units and minimize idle cycles.

These compiler optimizations for ILP are essential for maximizing the performance of modern processors with multiple execution units and deep pipelines. They transform high-level code into optimized machine code, ensuring that the processor can execute instructions concurrently and efficiently. However, it's important to note that the effectiveness of these optimizations can vary depending on the compiler's capabilities, the target architecture, and the nature of the code being optimized.

Chapter 9: Memory Systems and Caches

- ## Cache Organization and Design Principles

Cache memory is an integral part of modern computer architectures, designed to improve memory hierarchy and enhance overall system performance. Cache organization and design principles are critical for achieving efficient data access. Here's a detailed explanation of cache organization and key design principles:

Cache Organization:

Cache memory is a small, high-speed memory unit situated between the central processing unit (CPU) and main memory (RAM). Its primary purpose is to store frequently accessed data and instructions, reducing the time it takes for the CPU to fetch data from slower, larger main memory. Cache memory is organized into several key components:

1. **Cache Lines (Blocks):** The cache is divided into fixed-size blocks or lines, typically 32 to 128 bytes in size. Each block can store a portion of data from main memory.

2. **Cache Sets:** Cache lines are grouped into sets, and each set contains a fixed number of lines. The number of sets in a cache is determined by the cache's associativity. For example, in a 2-way set-associative cache, there are two lines per set.

3. **Cache Size:** The total capacity of the cache, measured in bytes, is a critical factor in cache organization. It determines how much data can be stored in the cache at any given time.

4. **Cache Mapping:** Cache mapping techniques determine how data is placed in cache sets. Common mapping techniques include direct-mapped (1-way set-associative), set-associative, and fully associative caches.

5. **Cache Replacement Policy:** When a cache is full and a new block needs to be loaded, the replacement policy determines which block is evicted to make room for the new one. Common replacement policies include LRU (Least Recently Used), FIFO (First-In-First-Out), and random replacement.

6. **Cache Write Policy:** Cache write policies dictate how writes to memory are handled. Common policies include write-through (writes to both cache and main memory) and write-back (writes to cache with later updates to main memory).

Cache Design Principles:

Effective cache design involves making decisions about cache size, associativity, and replacement policies to optimize data access patterns and minimize cache misses. Here are key design principles:

1. **Locality of Reference:** Cache design assumes the principle of locality, which suggests that programs tend to access a relatively small portion of memory frequently. Caches exploit temporal (reusing recently accessed data) and spatial (accessing nearby data) locality to reduce cache misses.

2. **Cache Size:** A larger cache typically leads to fewer cache misses, but it also increases access latency. Cache size decisions are influenced by cost, power consumption, and die area constraints.

3. **Cache Associativity:** Higher associativity allows for more flexible data placement, reducing the likelihood of cache conflicts (multiple data items mapping to the same set). However, increased associativity also comes with greater complexity and access latency.

4. **Replacement Policy:** The choice of replacement policy impacts cache performance. LRU is often considered optimal, but it can be costly to implement. Simpler policies like FIFO or random replacement may be more practical for some designs.

5. **Write Policy:** Write-back policies reduce main memory writes, but they require additional logic for tracking and updating modified data. Write-through policies ensure memory consistency but may increase memory traffic.

6. **Cache Coherency:** In multiprocessor systems, maintaining cache coherency is crucial to ensuring that multiple caches with copies of the same data remain consistent. Protocols like MESI (Modified, Exclusive, Shared, Invalid) help manage cache coherency.

7. **Cache Performance Metrics:** Evaluating cache performance involves measuring cache hit rate, miss rate, and overall access latency. Designers must balance these metrics to optimize overall system performance.

8. **Benchmarking and Simulation:** Cache design is often informed by benchmarking and simulation tools, which help assess how cache parameters affect real-world application performance.

Efficient cache organization and design principles are essential for achieving high-performance computing systems. Cache memory serves as a bridge between fast CPU execution and slower main memory, and optimizing its organization and operation is critical for achieving low-latency and high-throughput data access.

- ## Cache Coherency and Memory Consistency

Cache coherency and memory consistency are critical concepts in computer architecture, especially in multiprocessor and multicore systems where multiple CPUs or processing units share access to main memory. These concepts ensure that data remains consistent across different levels of the memory hierarchy and among different processors. Let's delve into each concept in detail:

Cache Coherency:

Cache coherency refers to the maintenance of data consistency across multiple caches and the main memory in a multiprocessor or multicore system. In such systems, each processor often has its own cache memory to reduce memory access latency. However, this caching can lead to the problem of stale or inconsistent data if not managed properly.

Key aspects of cache coherency:

1. **Shared Data:** Cache coherency is most relevant when multiple processors share access to the same data in main memory. When one processor writes to a shared memory location, other processors must be aware of and respond to this change to maintain data consistency.

2. **Cache States:** Cache lines in each cache can be in different states, depending on whether the data is valid and whether it has been modified compared to the main memory. Common cache states include "Modified," "Exclusive," "Shared," and "Invalid."

3. **Cache Coherency Protocols:** Cache coherency protocols, such as the MESI protocol (Modified, Exclusive, Shared, Invalid), define rules and mechanisms for maintaining cache coherence. These protocols ensure that caches update their states and communicate changes to other caches when necessary.

4. **Operations:** Cache coherency protocols handle various operations, including read (load) and write (store) operations. When a processor reads data, it must ensure that the data is not stale. When it writes data, it must notify other processors to invalidate or update their copies.

5. **Snooping vs. Directory-Based Protocols:** Two common approaches to cache coherency are snooping-based protocols and directory-based protocols. Snooping protocols involve each cache monitoring the bus for memory transactions, while directory-based protocols use a central directory to track data ownership and state.

6. **Coherency Traffic:** Cache coherency introduces additional traffic on the system's interconnect (bus or network) due to cache state updates and data transfers between caches.

Memory Consistency:

Memory consistency refers to the order in which memory operations (reads and writes) appear to occur for different processors or threads in a multiprocessor system. It defines the rules for how memory operations become visible to other processors and how they can be reordered.

Key aspects of memory consistency:

1. **Sequential Consistency:** Sequential consistency is a strong memory consistency model where all memory operations appear to occur in a single, global order. This model is conceptually simple but can limit optimization opportunities in parallel programs.

2. **Relaxed Consistency Models:** To improve performance, many systems employ relaxed memory consistency models that allow certain reorderings of memory operations. These models define precisely which reorderings are allowed.

3. **Memory Barriers and Synchronization:** Programmers use memory barriers (also known as memory fences or synchronization primitives) to enforce specific memory consistency constraints, ensuring that operations are visible in a desired order across different threads or processors.

4. **Data Races:** Violations of memory consistency can lead to data races, where multiple threads access and modify shared data without proper synchronization. Data races can result in unpredictable behavior and must be avoided.

5. **Happens-Before Relation:** In relaxed consistency models, the "happens-before" relation is used to define the order of memory operations. It ensures that certain operations appear to occur before others, providing a logical basis for reasoning about program behavior.

Understanding and managing memory consistency is crucial for parallel and concurrent programming. Different programming languages and frameworks provide mechanisms for specifying synchronization and memory ordering to ensure correct and predictable program behavior in multiprocessor systems.

In summary, cache coherency and memory consistency are fundamental concepts that ensure data remains correct and predictable in multiprocessor and multicore systems. Cache coherency protocols manage data consistency across caches, while memory consistency models define the order in which memory operations become visible to different processors or threads. These concepts are essential for the proper functioning of modern parallel and concurrent computing systems.

- Virtual Memory Systems and Paging.

Virtual memory systems and paging are fundamental concepts in computer architecture and operating systems, allowing for efficient memory management and the illusion of larger address spaces. Here's a detailed explanation of each concept:

Virtual Memory Systems:

Virtual memory is a memory management technique that provides the abstraction of a larger, contiguous, and more flexible address space to programs running on a computer. It allows programs to use more memory than physically available by swapping data between RAM (Random Access Memory) and secondary storage (usually a hard drive or SSD). Key aspects of virtual memory systems include:

1. **Address Translation:** Virtual memory uses address translation to map virtual addresses (used by programs) to physical addresses (locations in RAM). This mapping is maintained in a data structure known as the page table.

2. **Paging and Segmentation:** Two common approaches to virtual memory are paging and segmentation. In paging, memory is divided into fixed-size blocks called pages, while in segmentation, memory is divided into variable-sized segments based on the logical structure of the program.

3. **Demand Paging:** Virtual memory systems use demand paging, which means that pages or segments are loaded into RAM only when they are needed. This minimizes the amount of physical memory required at program startup.

4. **Page Faults:** When a program accesses a virtual address that is not currently in physical memory (a page fault), the operating system fetches the required page from secondary storage into RAM. Page replacement algorithms, such as LRU (Least Recently Used) or FIFO (First-In, First-Out), determine which pages to evict from RAM to make room for the new page.

5. **Protection and Isolation:** Virtual memory provides protection and isolation between processes. Each process has its own address space, and hardware mechanisms enforce access controls and prevent one process from accessing the memory of another.

6. **Address Space Layout Randomization (ASLR):** ASLR is a security feature of virtual memory systems that randomizes the locations of program code and data in memory. This makes it harder for attackers to exploit known memory vulnerabilities.

Paging:

Paging is a specific technique used in virtual memory systems to manage memory allocation and address translation. In a paged memory system, memory is divided into fixed-size blocks called pages, and both physical memory and virtual memory are divided into pages of the same size. Here's a detailed look at paging:

1. **Page Size:** The page size is a fixed power-of-2 size (e.g., 4 KB, 8 KB) that determines the granularity of memory allocation and address translation. All pages within a system are the same size.

2. **Page Table:** Each process has its own page table, which is used to translate virtual addresses into physical addresses. The page table contains entries that map virtual page numbers to physical page numbers or frame numbers.

3. **Page Table Entries:** A page table entry typically contains information such as the present/absent bit (indicating whether the page is in physical memory), permissions (read/write/execute), and additional control bits.

4. **Address Translation:** To translate a virtual address to a physical address, the processor splits the virtual address into two parts: a virtual page number and an offset within the page. The virtual page number is used as an index into the page table to retrieve the corresponding physical page number, which is then combined with the offset to form the physical address.

5. **Page Faults and Page Replacement:** When a page fault occurs, the operating system fetches the required page from secondary storage into an available physical page frame. If there are no available frames, a page replacement algorithm selects a victim page to be evicted from RAM.

6. **Benefits:** Paging provides efficient memory allocation, allows for flexible memory management, and simplifies address translation by using fixed-size pages. It also enables demand paging, where pages are loaded into RAM on demand.

Paging is widely used in modern operating systems and hardware architectures to provide efficient virtual memory management, enabling larger and more flexible address spaces for applications while minimizing the physical memory requirements.

- ### TLBs and Address Translation

Translation Lookaside Buffers (TLBs) are hardware caches used in modern computer architectures to accelerate the address translation process in virtual memory systems. They help bridge the gap between virtual and physical memory by reducing the time it takes to convert virtual addresses used by applications into corresponding physical addresses in RAM. Let's delve into TLBs and address translation in detail:

TLBs (Translation Lookaside Buffers):

1. **Purpose:** TLBs are designed to improve memory access performance by caching a subset of virtual-to-physical address translations. When a program generates a virtual address, the TLB checks whether the translation for that address is already cached. If it is, the TLB provides the corresponding physical address without needing to consult the page table in RAM, which is a slower operation.

2. **Cache Structure:** TLBs typically consist of multiple cache lines, each storing a virtual-to-physical address mapping (or translation) called a TLB entry. These entries are organized into sets, and each entry has fields for the virtual page number, physical page/frame number, and control bits (e.g., permissions and status bits).

3. **Address Translation Process:**

   - When the CPU generates a virtual memory address (e.g., during a load or store operation), the virtual address is sent to the TLB.

   - The TLB searches its cache for a matching virtual address (virtual page number).

   - If a match is found (a TLB hit), the corresponding physical page/frame number is retrieved, and the physical address is constructed by combining this number with the offset portion of the virtual address.

   - If there's no match (a TLB miss), the CPU proceeds to the next step.

4. **Handling TLB Misses:**

   - In case of a TLB miss, the CPU must consult the page table in RAM to obtain the translation.

   - The page table stores the complete mapping of virtual addresses to physical addresses. The page table entry for the virtual address is fetched, and the TLB is updated with this new entry.

   - Subsequent accesses to the same virtual address will now result in TLB hits as long as the entry remains cached in the TLB.

5. **Replacement Policy:** TLBs have a finite capacity, so when a TLB is full and a new entry is needed, a replacement policy (e.g., LRU or random replacement) determines which entry is evicted to make room for the new one.

6. **TLB Hierarchy:** Some systems employ a two-level TLB hierarchy, with a small, fast Level 1 (L1) TLB for frequently used translations and a larger, slower Level 2 (L2) TLB for less frequently accessed translations. This hierarchy helps balance access time and TLB capacity.

Address Translation in Detail:

Address translation in virtual memory systems involves the conversion of a virtual address generated by a program into a physical address in RAM. Here's a step-by-step overview:

1. **Generation of Virtual Address:** When a program or process running on a CPU accesses memory, it generates a virtual address. This virtual address typically consists of two parts: a virtual page number (VPN) and an offset within the page.

2. **TLB Lookup:** The virtual address is first checked against the TLB cache. If the TLB contains a matching translation, this is a TLB hit, and the corresponding physical page/frame number is retrieved from the TLB entry.

3. **Page Table Lookup (TLB Miss):** In case of a TLB miss, the virtual page number (VPN) is used to index the page table stored in RAM. The page table entry (PTE) corresponding to the VPN is fetched.

4. **Construction of Physical Address:** The retrieved physical page/frame number (from either the TLB or the page table) is combined with the offset within the page to construct the physical address. The offset remains unchanged, while the physical page/frame number replaces the virtual page number.

5. **Access to Physical Memory:** The physical address is then used to access the corresponding location in physical memory (RAM), allowing data or instructions to be read from or written to memory.

6. **Memory Protection and Permissions:** The memory management unit (MMU), which handles address translation, also enforces memory protection and access permissions. It checks whether the requested operation (e.g., read or write) is allowed based on the permissions specified in the page table entry.

Address translation plays a crucial role in virtual memory systems, enabling the isolation of processes, efficient use of physical memory, and providing the illusion of a large, contiguous address space to programs. TLBs are instrumental in speeding up this translation process by caching frequently used translations, reducing the need to access the slower main memory for each memory operation.

Chapter 10: Storage Systems and RAID

- ### Hard Disk Drives (HDD) vs. Solid-State Drives (SSD)

Hard Disk Drives (HDDs) and Solid-State Drives (SSDs) are two types of storage devices used in computers and other electronic devices. They differ significantly in terms of technology, performance, durability, and cost. Here's a detailed comparison of HDDs and SSDs:

1. Technology:

- **HDD (Hard Disk Drive):** HDDs use spinning magnetic disks or platters to store and retrieve data. Data is read and written using a mechanical arm with a read/write head that moves across the spinning platters.

- **SSD (Solid-State Drive):** SSDs use NAND flash memory to store data. Data is stored in memory cells that do not require moving parts to access, making them more akin to large-scale USB drives.

2. Performance:

- **HDD:** HDDs are slower than SSDs in terms of data access and transfer speeds. The mechanical components introduce latency, and data must be read sequentially, making random access slower.

- **SSD:** SSDs are significantly faster than HDDs. They provide much quicker data access and transfer speeds due to the absence of mechanical parts and the ability to read and write data simultaneously.

3. Durability:

- **HDD:** HDDs are more susceptible to physical damage because they have moving parts. Sudden shocks or drops can cause the read/write heads to crash into the platters, potentially leading to data loss.

- **SSD:** SSDs are more durable because they lack moving parts. They are better equipped to withstand physical shocks, making them a preferred choice for laptops and portable devices.

4. Power Consumption:

- **HDD:** HDDs consume more power than SSDs because they require the platters to spin and the read/write heads to move. This results in higher energy consumption and shorter battery life in laptops.

- **SSD:** SSDs are more power-efficient because they don't have moving parts. This makes them ideal for laptops and other battery-powered devices, as they consume less energy and extend battery life.

5. Noise and Vibration:

- **HDD:** HDDs generate noise and vibration due to the spinning platters and moving read/write heads. This can be a concern in quiet environments and may impact the lifespan of the drive.

- **SSD:** SSDs are silent and produce no noise or vibration because they lack moving parts. This makes them ideal for noise-sensitive environments and improves overall system reliability.

6. Size and Form Factor:

- **HDD:** HDDs are typically larger and heavier than SSDs. They come in standard sizes like 3.5 inches (desktop) and 2.5 inches (laptop).

- **SSD:** SSDs are smaller, lighter, and available in various form factors, including 2.5 inches (laptop), M.2, and U.2, making them suitable for a broader range of devices.

7. Cost:

- **HDD:** HDDs are generally more affordable than SSDs on a per-gigabyte basis, which makes them a cost-effective choice for large storage capacities.

- **SSD:** SSDs are more expensive than HDDs, especially when considering high-capacity drives. However, SSD prices have been decreasing over time.

8. Capacity:

- **HDD:** HDDs are available in larger capacities, making them the preferred choice for applications requiring massive storage, such as servers and network-attached storage (NAS) devices.

- **SSD:** SSDs offer a range of capacities, but they are typically smaller than HDDs for a similar price. SSD capacity has been increasing over the years but may not match the largest HDDs in terms of sheer storage space.

9. Reliability:

- **HDD:** HDDs have a limited lifespan due to mechanical wear and tear. Over time, the moving parts can degrade, potentially leading to drive failure.

- **SSD:** SSDs generally have a longer lifespan than HDDs because they lack mechanical components. However, the longevity of an SSD also depends on factors like write endurance, which can vary between different SSD models.

10. Heat Generation:

- **HDD:** HDDs generate more heat due to the spinning platters and moving parts, which may require additional cooling in some systems.

- **SSD:** SSDs generate less heat because they are primarily composed of non-moving electronic components.

In summary, HDDs and SSDs have distinct advantages and disadvantages. HDDs offer larger storage capacities at a lower cost per gigabyte but are slower, less durable, and more power-hungry. SSDs are faster, more durable, power-efficient, and compact but come at a higher cost per gigabyte. The choice between HDDs and SSDs depends on factors like performance requirements, budget, and the specific use case. Many modern systems use a combination of both, with an SSD for the operating system and frequently used applications, and an HDD for mass storage.

• RAID Levels and Data Striping

RAID (Redundant Array of Independent Disks) is a storage technology that combines multiple physical hard drives into a single logical unit to improve performance, redundancy, or a combination of both. RAID employs various techniques, including data striping, to achieve its objectives. Here's a detailed explanation of RAID levels and data striping:

RAID Levels:

There are several RAID levels, each with its own characteristics and use cases. The most common RAID levels include:

1. **RAID 0 (Striping):**

    - **Description:** RAID 0 uses data striping to spread data across multiple drives without providing redundancy. It enhances performance by allowing parallel read and write operations across all drives in the array.

    - **Benefits:** Improved read and write performance, especially for large files and data-intensive applications.

    - **Drawbacks:** No fault tolerance; if one drive fails, all data in the array is lost. RAID 0 is not suitable for critical data.

2. **RAID 1 (Mirroring):**

    - **Description:** RAID 1 duplicates data across two drives, creating a mirror copy. It offers data redundancy but doesn't improve read or write performance.

    - **Benefits:** High data redundancy; if one drive fails, data remains accessible from the other drive.

- **Drawbacks:** No performance improvement; storage capacity is effectively halved.

3. **RAID 5 (Striping with Parity):**

   - **Description:** RAID 5 uses data striping across multiple drives, with distributed parity information. This provides both performance improvements and fault tolerance.

   - **Benefits:** Improved performance and data redundancy; can tolerate the failure of one drive.

   - **Drawbacks:** Slower write performance due to parity calculations.

4. **RAID 6 (Striping with Dual Parity):**

   - **Description:** RAID 6 is similar to RAID 5 but includes two sets of parity information for enhanced fault tolerance. It can tolerate the failure of two drives.

   - **Benefits:** Robust fault tolerance; can withstand the failure of two drives.

   - **Drawbacks:** Slower write performance than RAID 5 due to additional parity calculations.

5. **RAID 10 (Combination of RAID 1 and RAID 0):**

   - **Description:** RAID 10 combines RAID 1 and RAID 0. It mirrors data across pairs of drives and then stripes data across those mirrored pairs.

   - **Benefits:** Excellent performance and fault tolerance; can withstand the failure of one drive in each mirrored pair.

   - **Drawbacks:** Requires a minimum of four drives, with half of the total capacity used for redundancy.

6. **RAID 50 and RAID 60 (Combination of RAID 5/6 and RAID 0):**

   - **Description:** These RAID levels combine the striping and parity features of RAID 5 or 6 with the performance benefits of RAID 0. They require a minimum of six drives (RAID 50) or eight drives (RAID 60).

   - **Benefits:** Balanced performance and fault tolerance.

   - **Drawbacks:** Complex configurations and higher hardware requirements.

Data Striping:

Data striping is a technique used in several RAID levels to improve performance by distributing data across multiple drives in the array. Here's how it works:

- **Striped Data Distribution:** When data is written to the RAID array, it is divided into chunks or stripes. These stripes are distributed across the drives in a round-robin fashion, allowing multiple drives to work in parallel when reading or writing data.

- **Performance Improvement:** Data striping enhances read and write performance, especially for large files and I/O-intensive applications. Multiple drives can be accessed simultaneously, reducing access times and improving data transfer rates.

- **No Redundancy:** In RAID 0, which uses pure data striping, there is no data redundancy. If one drive fails, all data in the array is lost. Data striping is primarily used for performance enhancement, not fault tolerance.

- **Combined with Parity:** Some RAID levels, such as RAID 5 and RAID 6, combine data striping with parity information to achieve both performance improvement and fault tolerance. This combination allows for improved performance while maintaining data redundancy.

- **Stripe Size:** The size of data stripes (stripe width) can be configured and varies depending on the RAID level and system requirements. Smaller stripe sizes can improve random I/O performance, while larger stripe sizes may be better for sequential I/O.

In summary, RAID levels and data striping are essential elements of storage management strategies. Each RAID level offers a unique balance of performance and data redundancy, making it suitable for specific use cases. Data striping enhances performance by distributing data across multiple drives, allowing for parallel access. However, it should be used in conjunction with appropriate RAID levels to provide data protection and fault tolerance, depending on the specific requirements of the storage environment.

- ## Storage Virtualization and Cloud Storage

Storage virtualization and cloud storage are two significant advancements in the field of data storage and management. They offer greater flexibility, scalability, and efficiency in handling data. Here's a detailed explanation of each concept:

Storage Virtualization:

Storage virtualization is a technology that abstracts physical storage resources, such as hard drives, RAID arrays, and network-attached storage (NAS) devices, and presents them as a single, unified storage pool to users and applications. This abstraction layer provides several benefits:

1. **Aggregation:** Storage virtualization aggregates diverse storage resources into a single pool, simplifying management and improving resource utilization. It allows organizations to make the most of their existing storage infrastructure.

2. **Centralized Management:** Users and administrators interact with a single, logical storage entity rather than dealing with individual storage devices. This simplifies provisioning, monitoring, and maintenance.

3. **Data Migration:** Storage virtualization enables non-disruptive data migrations. Data can be moved between different storage devices or tiers without affecting users or applications.

4. **Load Balancing:** Virtualization can distribute data across available storage devices, balancing workloads and preventing bottlenecks on specific devices.

5. **Improved Efficiency:** Thin provisioning, a storage virtualization feature, allows for the allocation of storage capacity as needed rather than pre-allocating space. This reduces wastage and optimizes storage utilization.

6. **Redundancy and Resilience:** Virtualization often includes features like mirroring and data replication, improving data redundancy and disaster recovery capabilities.

7. **Vendor Independence:** Virtualization solutions can work with storage devices from multiple vendors, reducing vendor lock-in and giving organizations more flexibility in choosing hardware.

8. **Simplified Scaling:** As storage needs grow, additional physical storage devices can be seamlessly integrated into the virtualized environment without significant disruption.

Cloud Storage:

Cloud storage involves storing data on remote servers, typically hosted and managed by third-party providers, accessible over the internet. It offers several advantages:

1. **Scalability:** Cloud storage is highly scalable, allowing organizations to increase or decrease storage capacity as needed. This eliminates the need to invest in and manage on-premises hardware.

2. **Cost Efficiency:** Users pay for cloud storage on a pay-as-you-go basis, avoiding upfront capital expenses. This cost model can be more economical for small and medium-sized businesses.

3. **Accessibility:** Cloud storage provides access to data from anywhere with an internet connection. This is valuable for remote work, collaboration, and disaster recovery.

4. **Redundancy:** Reputable cloud storage providers often have data centers in multiple geographic regions, ensuring data redundancy and disaster recovery capabilities.

5. **Security and Compliance:** Cloud providers invest in robust security measures and compliance certifications, addressing data protection and regulatory requirements.

6. **Automatic Backups:** Many cloud storage services offer automated backup solutions, reducing the risk of data loss.

7. **Data Sharing and Collaboration:** Cloud storage facilitates data sharing and collaboration among teams and individuals. Files can be easily shared, and collaborative tools are often integrated.

8. **Version Control:** Cloud storage solutions often include version control features, allowing users to revert to previous file versions.

9. **APIs and Integration:** Cloud storage providers offer APIs that enable integration with various applications and services, enhancing functionality and automation.

10. **Hybrid and Multi-Cloud:** Organizations can implement hybrid or multi-cloud strategies, combining on-premises storage with cloud storage resources for added flexibility.

It's worth noting that some organizations opt for a hybrid approach, combining storage virtualization and cloud storage. In this scenario, on-premises storage resources are virtualized and seamlessly integrated with cloud-based storage to create a unified storage environment. This approach provides the benefits of both technologies, allowing organizations to leverage their existing infrastructure while taking advantage of cloud storage's scalability and accessibility.

- ## Emerging Storage Technologies

Emerging storage technologies are continuously evolving to meet the growing demands for faster, more reliable, and more efficient data storage solutions. These technologies aim to address various challenges in data storage, such as increasing storage capacity, improving data access speeds, enhancing data durability, and reducing power consumption. Here are some of the prominent emerging storage technologies:

1. Non-Volatile Memory Express (NVMe):

Description: NVMe is a protocol designed to maximize the performance of solid-state drives (SSDs) by reducing latency and increasing data transfer rates. It leverages the high-speed PCIe (Peripheral Component Interconnect Express) interface, allowing SSDs to deliver significantly faster read and write speeds compared to traditional hard drives.

Benefits: Improved storage performance, reduced latency, and increased scalability. NVMe SSDs are commonly used in data centers, workstations, and high-performance computing environments.

2. Storage-Class Memory (SCM):

Description: SCM, also known as persistent memory, is a type of memory technology that bridges the gap between traditional volatile RAM and non-volatile storage devices like SSDs. It offers byte-addressable access and near-DRAM speeds while retaining data even when power is removed.

Benefits: SCM provides low-latency, high-speed storage with the ability to withstand power failures, making it suitable for applications that require both performance and data persistence.

3. 3D NAND Flash Memory:

Description: 3D NAND flash memory is an advancement in NAND flash technology that stacks memory cells vertically in multiple layers, increasing storage capacity while reducing the physical footprint of SSDs. This technology allows for higher storage densities and lower costs per gigabyte.

Benefits: Increased storage capacity, improved reliability, and cost-effectiveness. 3D NAND is widely used in consumer electronics, data centers, and enterprise storage solutions.

4. Storage Class and Computational Storage:

Description: Storage class memory (SCM) and computational storage are concepts that combine storage and processing capabilities within the same hardware device. Computational storage devices offload processing tasks from the CPU, enabling data processing to occur closer to the data storage location.

Benefits: Reduced data movement, lower latency, improved data processing efficiency, and enhanced scalability. These technologies are particularly relevant for data-intensive and analytics workloads.

5. Optane Technology (Optane SSDs):

Description: Optane is Intel's brand for a class of 3D XPoint non-volatile memory and SSD products. It combines characteristics of both NAND flash and traditional DRAM, offering high-speed data access with persistent storage.

Benefits: Optane SSDs provide low-latency, high-IOPS (Input/Output Operations Per Second) performance, making them suitable for a wide range of applications, including databases and caching.

6. Shingled Magnetic Recording (SMR):

Description: SMR is a magnetic storage technology that increases data storage density by overlapping or "shingling" data tracks on a hard disk drive (HDD). While it boosts capacity, it requires specialized firmware and file systems to manage data writes effectively.

Benefits: Enhanced storage density, cost-effectiveness, and increased HDD capacities. SMR HDDs are commonly used for archival and cold storage.

7. DNA Data Storage:

Description: DNA data storage is an emerging biotechnology approach that encodes digital data in the form of DNA molecules. DNA offers extremely high data density, long-term stability, and resistance to environmental factors.

Benefits: Exceptional data density, long-term data preservation, and potential for storing vast amounts of data in a tiny volume. However, it is still in the experimental phase and not yet practical for mainstream use.

8. Quantum Storage:

Description: Quantum storage is an emerging field that explores the use of quantum mechanics to store and retrieve data. Quantum storage devices, such as quantum memory and quantum hard drives, leverage the properties of quantum bits (qubits) for ultra-secure and high-capacity data storage.

Benefits: Quantum storage has the potential to revolutionize data security and storage capacity. However, it is in the early stages of research and development.

These emerging storage technologies are reshaping the landscape of data storage and management. They offer a range of benefits, from improved performance and capacity to increased data durability and innovative storage approaches. As these technologies mature, they are likely to play a crucial role in addressing the evolving storage needs of various industries and applications.

Chapter 11: Networking and Interconnects

- Network Topologies and Communication Protocols

Network topologies and communication protocols are fundamental concepts in computer networking that define how devices are connected in a network and how they communicate with each other. Let's explore each of these concepts in detail:

Network Topologies:

Network topology refers to the physical or logical layout of devices and the way they are interconnected in a network. Different network topologies have distinct advantages and disadvantages, depending on factors like scalability, fault tolerance, and cost. Here are some common network topologies:

1. **Bus Topology:**

    - **Description:** In a bus topology, all devices are connected to a central cable (the "bus"). Data is transmitted as electrical signals along the bus, and devices receive and filter data based on their unique address.

    - **Advantages:** Simplicity, low cost, and easy installation for small networks.

    - **Disadvantages:** Limited scalability, a single point of failure (the central cable), and reduced performance as more devices are added.

2. **Star Topology:**

    - **Description:** In a star topology, all devices are connected to a central hub or switch. Data flows through the hub, which manages data traffic between devices.

    - **Advantages:** High scalability, easy fault detection, and the failure of one device does not affect the rest of the network.

    - **Disadvantages:** Higher cost due to the central hub, potential bottlenecks at the hub, and the hub itself as a single point of failure.

3. **Ring Topology:**

    - **Description:** In a ring topology, devices are connected in a closed loop. Data travels in a circular path from one device to the next until it reaches its destination.

    - **Advantages:** Balanced data traffic, no central hub, and predictable performance.

    - **Disadvantages:** Limited scalability, the failure of one device can disrupt the entire network, and additional mechanisms are required to prevent data from circulating endlessly.

4. **Mesh Topology:**

    - **Description:** In a mesh topology, every device is connected to every other device, forming a fully interconnected network. Mesh networks can be either partial (some devices are selectively interconnected) or full (every device connects to every other).

    - **Advantages:** High fault tolerance (redundant paths), robustness, and the ability to handle heavy data traffic.

    - **Disadvantages:** High cost (due to numerous connections), complexity in design and management, and difficult scalability for full mesh networks.

5. **Hybrid Topology:**

   - **Description:** A hybrid topology combines two or more of the above-mentioned topologies. For example, a network might have a star topology within individual departments and a backbone ring connecting department hubs.

   - **Advantages:** Flexibility to meet specific network requirements and balance between cost, scalability, and fault tolerance.

   - **Disadvantages:** Complexity in design and management, which can vary depending on the specific hybrid configuration.

Communication Protocols:

Communication protocols define the rules and conventions for data exchange between devices in a network. They encompass various layers, each responsible for specific aspects of communication. The OSI (Open Systems Interconnection) model and the TCP/IP model are commonly used as reference models for understanding networking protocols. Here are key layers and protocols in these models:

1. **Physical Layer:**

   - **Protocols:** Ethernet, USB, Bluetooth, and Wi-Fi (802.11 standards) for wired and wireless physical connections.

2. **Data Link Layer:**

   - **Protocols:** Ethernet (IEEE 802.3), Wi-Fi (IEEE 802.11), and Point-to-Point Protocol (PPP) for link establishment, error detection, and addressing.

3. **Network Layer:**

   - **Protocols:** Internet Protocol (IP) for logical addressing and routing (IPv4 and IPv6), and Internet Control Message Protocol (ICMP) for error reporting.

4. **Transport Layer:**

   - **Protocols:** Transmission Control Protocol (TCP) for reliable, connection-oriented communication, and User Datagram Protocol (UDP) for connectionless, best-effort communication.

5. **Session Layer, Presentation Layer, and Application Layer:**

   - **Protocols:** A wide range of application-specific protocols like Hypertext Transfer Protocol (HTTP) for web browsing, Simple Mail Transfer Protocol (SMTP) for email, and File Transfer Protocol (FTP) for file transfer.

6. **Routing Protocols:**

   - **Protocols:** Routing Information Protocol (RIP), Open Shortest Path First (OSPF), and Border Gateway Protocol (BGP) for routing and path selection in routers.

7. **Security Protocols:**

- **Protocols:** Secure Sockets Layer (SSL)/Transport Layer Security (TLS) for secure data transmission, IPsec for secure IP communication, and Virtual Private Network (VPN) protocols for secure network connections.

8. **Application Layer Protocols for Specific Use Cases:**

- **Examples:** Simple Network Management Protocol (SNMP) for network management, Post Office Protocol (POP) and Internet Message Access Protocol (IMAP) for email retrieval, and Domain Name System (DNS) for hostname-to-IP address resolution.

These protocols work together in a layered fashion to ensure efficient and reliable communication between devices on a network. The choice of communication protocols depends on the specific requirements and applications of the network, ensuring that data is transmitted accurately and securely.

- ## Interconnection Networks: Buses, Crossbars, Meshes

Interconnection networks are a crucial component of computer systems and supercomputers, facilitating communication between various processing elements, memory modules, and peripheral devices. Different interconnection topologies are employed, including buses, crossbars, and meshes, each with its own advantages and limitations. Here's a detailed explanation of these interconnection networks:

1. Bus-Based Interconnection:

A bus is a shared communication channel that connects multiple devices on a computer system. It's one of the simplest and most commonly used interconnection networks, especially in small-scale systems.

- **Description:** In a bus-based system, all devices share a single communication pathway called a bus. Devices are connected to the bus through interfaces. Data and control signals travel along the bus, and devices use these signals to communicate with each other.

- **Advantages:**

  - Simplicity and low cost.

  - Suitable for small-scale systems.

  - Well-suited for systems with a limited number of devices.

- **Limitations:**

  - Limited scalability: As more devices are added, the bus can become a bottleneck, leading to reduced performance.

  - Shared bandwidth: All devices compete for access to the bus, potentially causing contention and delays.

  - Limited distance: Buses are typically limited in length, which can constrain the physical layout of the system.

2. Crossbar Interconnection:

A crossbar switch is a more sophisticated interconnection network that provides a dedicated connection between every pair of input and output ports. It's commonly used in high-performance computing systems.

- **Description:** In a crossbar interconnection, a grid of switches forms a matrix, allowing each input to connect directly to any output. This non-blocking architecture ensures that devices can communicate simultaneously without contention.

- **Advantages:**

    - Full connectivity: Crossbars provide a direct connection between any input and any output, eliminating contention.

    - High performance and low latency: Devices can communicate independently without waiting for access to a shared bus.

    - Scalability: Crossbars can scale to accommodate a large number of devices.

- **Limitations:**

    - Complexity and cost: Crossbar switches can be expensive to implement, especially in large-scale systems.

    - Power consumption: The large number of switches can lead to higher power consumption.

    - Limited fault tolerance: If a switch or connection fails, it can disrupt the entire system.

3. Mesh-Based Interconnection:

Mesh interconnection networks are often used in multiprocessor systems and supercomputers. They are based on a grid-like structure where devices are interconnected in a systematic manner.

- **Description:** In a mesh-based interconnection network, devices are organized in rows and columns, forming a grid. Each device is connected to its neighbors in a predefined manner. Data can be routed through multiple devices to reach its destination.

- **Advantages:**

    - Scalability: Meshes can scale to accommodate a large number of devices.

    - Fault tolerance: Redundant paths can be used to bypass failed devices, improving fault tolerance.

    - Good balance between performance and cost: Meshes offer reasonable performance without the complexity of crossbar switches.

- **Limitations:**

    - Limited connectivity: Devices can communicate directly with their immediate neighbors but may require multiple hops to reach distant devices.

    - Moderate complexity: While less complex than crossbar switches, mesh networks still require careful design and routing algorithms.

Variations of Meshes:

- **Torus:** A torus is a variation of a mesh network where the edges are connected to form a loop. This eliminates the edge devices' boundary effects and provides more uniform communication paths.

- **Hypercube:** A hypercube network is a mesh where each device is connected to a logarithmic number of other devices. It is commonly used in parallel computing environments.

The choice of interconnection network depends on the specific requirements of the system, including the number of devices, desired performance, fault tolerance, and cost considerations. In practice, many high-performance systems use a combination of these interconnection topologies to optimize communication and balance cost-effectiveness.

- ## Network-on-Chip (NoC) and High-Performance Interconnects

Network-on-Chip (NoC) and high-performance interconnects are advanced technologies used in modern computer systems and microprocessors to facilitate efficient communication among various on-chip components and processors. They are particularly crucial in complex, multi-core, and many-core processors, as well as in systems-on-chip (SoCs). Let's explore these concepts in detail:

1. Network-on-Chip (NoC):

Network-on-Chip (NoC) is an advanced communication architecture designed to replace traditional bus-based and point-to-point interconnects within an integrated circuit (IC) or chip. It treats on-chip communication like a network, with routers, switches, and communication links, allowing for scalable and efficient data transfer among different IP cores, processors, memory blocks, and other functional units on the chip. Here's an in-depth look at NoC:

- **Components of NoC:**

  - **Routers:** Routers in a NoC serve as the intermediaries for data packets. They determine the best path for data to traverse the network based on routing algorithms, ensuring efficient communication between source and destination.

  - **Switches:** Switches connect multiple routers and facilitate network scalability. They help route data between different network segments and provide redundancy for improved fault tolerance.

  - **Communication Links:** Communication links represent the physical connections between routers and switches. These links can vary in terms of bandwidth, latency, and power consumption.

- **Advantages of NoC:**

  - **Scalability:** NoCs can easily scale to accommodate an increasing number of IP cores and other components on a chip, making them suitable for multi-core and many-core processors.

  - **Reduced Latency:** NoC architectures can provide lower latency compared to traditional bus-based interconnects, as data can take multiple paths to reach its destination quickly.

  - **Improved Bandwidth:** NoCs offer increased bandwidth, enabling multiple transactions to occur simultaneously, which is critical for high-performance computing.

- **Power Efficiency:** NoCs can be designed to minimize power consumption by using advanced power management techniques like voltage scaling and dynamic routing.

- **Challenges:**

  - **Complex Design:** Designing a NoC can be complex and challenging due to the need for efficient routing algorithms, fault tolerance mechanisms, and power optimization strategies.

  - **Latency Variability:** While NoCs can reduce average latency, they may introduce variability in latency due to packet routing and contention, which needs to be carefully managed.

  - **Verification and Debugging:** Verifying and debugging NoC designs can be more complex than traditional interconnects.

2. High-Performance Interconnects:

High-performance interconnects refer to advanced communication technologies used to connect various components in a computer system, including processors, memory, accelerators, and input/output (I/O) devices. These interconnects are designed to meet the increasing demands for bandwidth, low latency, and energy efficiency in modern computing systems. Here are some key elements of high-performance interconnects:

- **High-Speed Data Links:** High-performance interconnects often use high-speed serial data links, such as PCIe (Peripheral Component Interconnect Express), Ethernet, InfiniBand, and others, to achieve high data transfer rates.

- **Low-Latency Routing:** To minimize communication delays, high-performance interconnects employ low-latency routing algorithms that determine the quickest path for data to travel between source and destination.

- **Advanced Protocols:** These interconnects often use advanced communication protocols that provide features like flow control, error correction, quality of service (QoS), and virtualization to ensure efficient and reliable data transfer.

- **Scalability:** High-performance interconnects are designed with scalability in mind, allowing them to be used in both small-scale systems and large-scale data centers or supercomputers.

- **Remote Direct Memory Access (RDMA):** RDMA technology allows devices to read and write data in remote memory without involving the CPU, reducing CPU overhead and improving data transfer efficiency.

- **Topology Flexibility:** High-performance interconnects can support various network topologies, including fat-tree, hypercube, and others, to optimize network architecture for specific workloads.

- **Energy Efficiency:** Energy-efficient design is a crucial aspect of high-performance interconnects, especially for mobile and battery-powered devices.

These advanced interconnect technologies are essential for achieving high-performance computing, data-intensive applications, and efficient data movement in modern computer systems, data centers, and supercomputers. They are also critical for enabling technologies like artificial intelligence (AI), machine learning, and big data analytics, where rapid data exchange between processing units and memory is paramount.

- ## Parallel Computing and Network Challenges

Parallel Computing:

Parallel computing refers to the simultaneous execution of multiple tasks or processes to solve a problem. It is used to increase computational speed and efficiency by dividing a problem into smaller parts and processing them concurrently. Parallel computing is essential in various fields, including scientific simulations, data analysis, and artificial intelligence. However, it comes with its own set of challenges:

1. **Amdahl's Law:** Amdahl's Law states that the speedup gained from parallelization is limited by the fraction of the program that cannot be parallelized (the "serial fraction"). As the number of processors increases, the serial fraction becomes the bottleneck, limiting the potential speedup.

2. **Load Balancing:** In parallel computing, distributing work evenly among processors is critical for efficient execution. Load imbalance, where some processors finish work much earlier than others, can lead to idle processors and reduced efficiency.

3. **Data Dependency:** Parallel tasks often need to share data. Managing data dependencies, where one task relies on the output of another, can be complex. Synchronization mechanisms like locks and barriers can introduce overhead and potential bottlenecks.

4. **Scalability:** Scalability refers to a system's ability to handle an increasing number of processors or nodes efficiently. Achieving good scalability can be challenging, especially for algorithms that have inherent limitations in parallelization.

5. **Communication Overhead:** As the number of processors increases, communication between them can introduce overhead. Minimizing communication, optimizing message passing, and using efficient communication libraries are crucial for reducing this overhead.

6. **Fault Tolerance:** In large parallel systems, the probability of hardware failures increases. Implementing fault-tolerant mechanisms, such as redundancy and checkpoint/restart, is essential to ensure system reliability.

7. **Programming Complexity:** Writing parallel code is more complex than sequential code. Parallel programmers must consider thread safety, race conditions, and deadlocks. Learning and debugging parallel code can be challenging.

Network Challenges:

Parallel computing often relies on high-speed interconnects and networks to facilitate communication between processors or nodes. Network challenges in this context encompass various issues:

1. **Latency:** Latency is the time it takes for a message to travel from the sender to the receiver. High latency can significantly impact the performance of parallel applications, especially those that require frequent communication.

2. **Bandwidth:** Bandwidth is the data transfer rate of a network. In parallel computing, applications may require high bandwidth for efficient data exchange. Inadequate bandwidth can lead to communication bottlenecks.

3. **Congestion:** In networks with multiple users or applications, congestion can occur when too many data packets compete for limited network resources. Congestion can lead to packet loss, increased latency, and reduced throughput.

4. **Scalability:** Network scalability is the ability to accommodate an increasing number of nodes or users without degrading performance. Scalable network design is critical in large parallel systems.

5. **Reliability:** Network failures or interruptions can disrupt parallel computations. Redundancy, fault tolerance, and quality-of-service (QoS) mechanisms are essential for maintaining network reliability.

6. **Security:** Parallel computing often involves the transfer of sensitive data. Ensuring the security and privacy of data during transmission is crucial to protect against cyber threats.

7. **Network Topology:** The choice of network topology, such as bus, ring, mesh, or tree, can impact communication efficiency and fault tolerance. Selecting an appropriate topology is essential.

8. **Network Protocols:** Efficient network protocols and communication libraries are essential for optimizing data exchange in parallel applications. Choosing the right protocol can significantly affect performance.

9. **Data Movement:** In parallel computing, moving data between nodes or processors is a fundamental operation. Minimizing unnecessary data movement and optimizing data transfer mechanisms are key challenges.

Addressing these challenges in parallel computing and network design requires a combination of hardware innovations, software optimizations, and careful system architecture planning. Researchers and engineers continually work to develop solutions that improve the efficiency and scalability of parallel systems while mitigating the associated challenges.

Chapter 12: Energy-Efficient Architectures

- Power Consumption in Computer Systems

Power consumption in computer systems is a critical aspect of modern computing due to its impact on energy efficiency, environmental concerns, and operational costs. Understanding power consumption and its management is essential for designing energy-efficient computer systems. Let's explore power consumption in computer systems in detail:

1. Components of Power Consumption:

Power consumption in computer systems can be broken down into several key components:

a. Active Power (Dynamic Power):

- **Description:** Active power is the power consumed by the computer's components when they are actively performing computations or executing tasks. It primarily includes the power used by the CPU, GPU, memory, and other active electronic components.

- **Example:** When you play a graphics-intensive video game, the CPU and GPU work at high clock speeds and voltage levels, resulting in increased active power consumption.

- **Factors Influencing Active Power:**

  - **Clock Frequency:** Higher clock speeds generally result in higher active power consumption.

  - **Voltage:** Increasing voltage to components also leads to increased power consumption.

  - **Workload:** Intensive computational tasks, such as gaming or scientific simulations, demand more active power.

b. Standby Power (Static Power):

- **Description:** Standby power, also known as static power or leakage power, is the power consumed by components when they are powered on but not actively performing tasks. It's the power consumed to maintain the state of the system.

- **Example:** Even when your computer is in sleep mode, it consumes standby power to keep the RAM contents intact and enable a quick wake-up when you resume work.

- **Factors Influencing Standby Power:**

  - **Process Technology:** Smaller semiconductor process technologies tend to have lower standby power due to reduced leakage currents.

  - **Component Design:** Advanced power management techniques and low-power states can minimize standby power.

c. Peripheral Power:

- **Description:** Peripheral devices such as hard drives, optical drives, and external devices also consume power. The power consumed by these devices can vary widely.

- **Example:** When a hard drive spins up to access data, it consumes additional power. External devices like USB drives and monitors also draw power from the computer.

- **Factors Influencing Peripheral Power:**

  - **Device Type:** Different types of peripherals have different power requirements. For example, hard drives consume more power during spin-up and data access.

2. Managing Power Consumption:

Efficiently managing power consumption in computer systems is critical for various reasons, including cost savings, environmental concerns, and extending the lifespan of hardware. Here are some strategies for managing power consumption:

a. Power Management Features:

- **Advanced Configuration and Power Interface (ACPI):** ACPI is a standard that allows the operating system to control power management features of the hardware. It enables features like sleep states (e.g., S3 for suspend to RAM) and CPU frequency scaling.

- **Example:** When your computer is idle, ACPI can trigger the CPU to lower its clock speed and voltage, reducing active power consumption.

b. Dynamic Voltage and Frequency Scaling (DVFS):

- **Description:** DVFS allows components like the CPU and GPU to adjust their voltage and frequency dynamically based on workload. This reduces power consumption during periods of lower activity.

- **Example:** When you're browsing the internet or reading emails, DVFS can reduce the CPU's clock speed and voltage to save power.

c. Sleep and Hibernation Modes:

- **Description:** Sleep and hibernation modes allow the system to enter low-power states when idle. Sleep states (e.g., S3) keep the system in a low-power state while allowing quick wake-up, while hibernation saves the system state to disk and shuts down completely.

- **Example:** When you close the laptop lid or leave your desktop idle, it can enter sleep mode to conserve power. In hibernation, the system saves its state to resume later with minimal power consumption.

d. Power-efficient Hardware Components:

- **Description:** Selecting power-efficient hardware components, such as CPUs with lower TDP (Thermal Design Power) ratings, energy-efficient memory modules, and SSDs instead of traditional HDDs, can significantly reduce power consumption.

e. Monitoring and Optimization:

- **Description:** Use power monitoring tools and system utilities to identify power-hungry processes and applications. You can then optimize them for better energy efficiency.

3. Environmental and Cost Considerations:

a. Energy Efficiency: Energy-efficient computing not only reduces operational costs but also lowers the carbon footprint, contributing to environmental sustainability.

Example: Data centers and cloud providers are adopting energy-efficient technologies to reduce the environmental impact of their operations.

b. Total Cost of Ownership (TCO): Lowering power consumption can reduce the TCO of computing systems, including electricity costs and maintenance expenses.

Example: Businesses and organizations often assess TCO when choosing energy-efficient computing solutions to optimize their budgets.

c. Green Computing: Organizations and data centers are increasingly adopting green computing practices to minimize power consumption, waste, and environmental impact.

Example: Tech companies are designing products with energy-efficient components and recyclable materials, aligning with green computing principles.

4. Future Trends:

As technology advances, power consumption remains a significant concern. Some future trends in power consumption management include:

a. Energy-efficient Processors: Continued development of processors with improved energy efficiency and power management features.

Example: Modern CPUs are designed to operate efficiently at lower power levels while delivering high performance.

b. Alternative Power Sources: Exploration of alternative power sources, such as renewable energy, for data centers and large computing facilities.

Example: Data centers are increasingly adopting renewable energy sources to power their operations and reduce their carbon footprint.

c. More Efficient Cooling: Improved cooling technologies to dissipate heat efficiently, reducing the need for power-hungry cooling solutions.

Example: Liquid cooling and advanced thermal management techniques are being adopted to increase energy efficiency in data centers.

d. Energy-efficient Algorithms: Development of algorithms that are optimized for energy efficiency, particularly in applications like artificial intelligence and machine learning.

Example: Researchers are working on energy-efficient AI algorithms that can run on low-power hardware devices.

In conclusion, power consumption in computer systems is a multifaceted concern with economic, environmental, and operational implications. Managing power consumption through hardware selection, power management features, and energy-efficient practices is crucial in today's computing landscape to achieve sustainability and cost savings while maintaining computing performance and reliability.

- ## Dynamic Voltage and Frequency Scaling (DVFS)

Dynamic Voltage and Frequency Scaling (DVFS) is a power management technique used in computer systems to optimize energy efficiency by dynamically adjusting the voltage and clock frequency of a processor or other hardware components based on workload and performance requirements. This technique allows hardware to operate at lower power levels during periods of low demand and scale up to higher performance when needed. Here, we'll delve into DVFS in detail:

1. How DVFS Works:

DVFS is primarily implemented in CPUs and GPUs but can also be applied to other hardware components, such as memory and peripherals. The fundamental idea behind DVFS is to vary the operating voltage and clock frequency of these components to match the current workload, thus reducing power consumption when full performance is not required.

2. Key Components of DVFS:

a. **Voltage Regulator:** The voltage regulator supplies power to the processor or component. It can dynamically adjust the voltage provided based on the DVFS algorithm's commands.

b. **Frequency Scaling**: Frequency scaling involves adjusting the clock frequency of the component. Lowering the clock frequency reduces the number of instructions executed per second, decreasing power consumption.

c. **DVFS Algorithm**: A DVFS algorithm, often implemented in hardware or firmware, monitors the workload and system conditions. It decides when and by how much to adjust the voltage and frequency.

3. Modes of DVFS:

a. **Static Voltage and Frequency Scaling**: In this mode, the operating voltage and frequency are set at specific levels, typically during system boot, and remain constant until the system is powered down or restarted. It does not dynamically adapt to workload changes.

b. **Dynamic Voltage and Frequency Scaling (Dynamic Scaling):** This is the most common mode of DVFS. In this mode, the hardware continuously monitors system conditions and adjusts the voltage and frequency on-the-fly based on real-time workload requirements.

4. Benefits of DVFS:

a. **Energy Efficiency**: DVFS reduces power consumption, making computing systems more energy-efficient. It is especially valuable in mobile devices and laptops where battery life is crucial.

b. **Thermal Management**: By reducing power consumption during periods of lower activity, DVFS helps manage thermal issues and prevents hardware from overheating.

c. **Extended Component Lifespan**: Operating components at lower voltage and frequency levels can extend their lifespan by reducing wear and tear associated with higher power states.

5. **Challenges and Considerations**:

a. **Workload Detection:** Accurate workload detection is crucial for effective DVFS operation. Algorithms must correctly identify periods of high and low activity.

b. **Responsiveness**: DVFS algorithms need to be responsive to workload changes. Delayed responses can impact system performance.

c. **Trade-off Between Performance and Energy Efficiency:** Aggressive DVFS settings may prioritize energy efficiency at the expense of performance. Striking the right balance is essential.

d. **Voltage-Frequency Dependency:** The relationship between voltage and frequency is not linear. Lowering voltage may require reducing the frequency to maintain stability.

e. **Compatibility**: Some software applications may not work optimally with DVFS-enabled hardware, so compatibility testing is necessary.

6. **Practical Applications**:

a. **Mobile Devices:** DVFS is widely used in smartphones and tablets to optimize battery life without sacrificing performance.

b. **Data Centers:** In large data centers, DVFS helps manage power consumption, reduce cooling costs, and improve the energy efficiency of servers.

c. **Laptops and Ultrabooks:** DVFS allows laptops to balance performance and battery life by adjusting power consumption based on user activity.

d. **Embedded Systems:** In embedded systems, DVFS is used to manage power consumption in devices like IoT sensors and industrial controllers.

7. **Operating System Support:**

Most modern operating systems, including Windows, macOS, and Linux, have built-in support for DVFS. They interact with the hardware's DVFS controller to manage voltage and frequency adjustments transparently to users and applications. Dynamic Voltage and Frequency Scaling (DVFS) is a vital power management technique that plays a crucial role in improving energy efficiency, extending battery life, and managing thermal concerns in computer systems. It's a versatile tool that can adapt to a wide range of computing environments, from mobile devices to data centers, helping strike the right balance between performance and energy conservation.

- ## Power Management Techniques

Power management techniques are strategies and methods used to optimize the usage of electrical power in electronic devices and systems. These techniques are crucial in today's world where energy efficiency and conservation are essential to reduce environmental impact and extend the battery life of portable devices. Below, I'll detail some common power management techniques:

1. **Dynamic Voltage and Frequency Scaling (DVFS):**

    - DVFS adjusts the voltage and frequency of a microprocessor or other components dynamically based on the workload. When the workload is low, the voltage and frequency are reduced to save power, and when the workload increases, they are increased for better performance.

2. **Sleep Modes:**

    - Electronic devices often have various sleep or low-power modes. These modes reduce power consumption by shutting down or reducing the power to certain components when they are not actively in use. Common sleep modes include:

        - **Idle State**: Reducing the clock frequency and voltage when the device is not in use.

        - **Standby or Sleep Mode**: Turning off non-essential components while keeping essential functions active.

        - **Hibernation**: Saving the current state to non-volatile memory and then powering off completely.

3. **Clock Gating:**

    - Clock gating involves disabling clock signals to specific parts of a circuit when they are not needed. This prevents unnecessary power consumption in inactive sections of a device.

4. **Cache Management:**

    - Caches are used to store frequently accessed data for faster retrieval. Proper cache management, such as flushing or shutting down cache lines when not needed, can save power.

5. **Dynamic Power Management (DPM):**

    - DPM involves dynamically enabling or disabling various components or subsystems based on workload and usage patterns. For instance, turning off unused peripherals, like Wi-Fi or Bluetooth, can save power.

6. **Energy-Efficient Algorithms:**

- Software-level optimizations can significantly impact power consumption. Using efficient algorithms and data structures can reduce the computational workload and, in turn, power consumption.

7. **LED Brightness Control:**

   - In devices with LED displays, adjusting the brightness of the LEDs based on ambient light conditions or user preferences can save power.

8. **Battery Management:**

   - Battery management techniques include monitoring and regulating battery voltage and current to ensure optimal charging and discharging, as well as preventing overcharging or over-discharging.

9. **Power-Efficient Hardware Design:**

   - Hardware-level design considerations, such as using low-power components, designing for low leakage currents, and minimizing signal switching, can all contribute to power efficiency.

10. **Thermal Management:**

    - Keeping electronic components within their specified temperature ranges is crucial for power efficiency. Excessive heat can lead to increased power consumption, so thermal management techniques like heat sinks and fans are used.

11. **Predictive Algorithms:**

    - Predictive algorithms can anticipate the power requirements of a device based on user behavior and adjust power management strategies accordingly.

12. **Voltage Regulation:**

    - Efficient voltage regulation techniques ensure that electronic components receive a stable power supply without wasting excess energy as heat.

13. **Smart Power Grids:**

    - In large-scale power management systems, like data centers, implementing smart power grids can optimize power distribution and reduce energy waste.

14. **Power Monitoring and Reporting:**

    - Continuous monitoring of power usage and providing feedback to users can encourage more power-efficient behavior.

15. **Energy Harvesting:**

    - In some cases, devices can harvest energy from the environment, such as solar panels or kinetic energy scavengers, to power themselves, reducing reliance on traditional power sources.

Effective power management techniques vary depending on the specific application and constraints. Engineers and designers must carefully select and implement these techniques to meet the power efficiency goals of their devices or systems.

- Green Computing and Sustainable Design

Green computing and sustainable design are approaches that aim to minimize the environmental impact of information technology (IT) and electronic systems. These practices focus on reducing energy consumption, minimizing electronic waste, and promoting environmentally responsible manufacturing processes. Below, I'll provide a detailed overview of green computing and sustainable design:

Green Computing:

1. **Energy Efficiency:**

    - **Power Management:** Green computing emphasizes the use of power management techniques such as sleep modes, dynamic voltage and frequency scaling, and intelligent power distribution to reduce energy consumption in electronic devices.

    - **Energy-Efficient Hardware:** Selecting energy-efficient components and designs for servers, desktops, laptops, and data centers is crucial. This includes low-power processors, energy-efficient power supplies, and cooling systems.

    - **Renewable Energy:** Implementing renewable energy sources, such as solar or wind power, to provide electricity for data centers and other IT infrastructure.

2. **Virtualization:**

    - **Server Virtualization:** Consolidating multiple servers onto a single physical server using virtualization technology reduces hardware requirements, saving energy and space.

    - **Desktop Virtualization:** Centralized desktop virtualization can reduce the energy consumption of individual desktop computers.

3. **Cloud Computing:**

    - Cloud computing allows for resource sharing and allocation, which can optimize server utilization and reduce the need for individual organizations to maintain large data centers.

4. **Efficient Cooling:** Proper data center design with efficient cooling systems can significantly reduce energy consumption, as cooling can account for a substantial portion of data center energy use.

5. **E-Waste Management:**

    - Encouraging responsible disposal and recycling of electronic waste is a key aspect of green computing. This includes proper recycling and disposal of old computers, monitors, and other electronic equipment.

6. **Lifecycle Assessment:** Assessing the environmental impact of IT products throughout their entire lifecycle, from manufacturing and use to disposal, helps identify opportunities for improvement.

Sustainable Design:

1. **Material Selection:**

- Sustainable design involves choosing materials that have a minimal environmental impact, such as recycled or recyclable materials. Additionally, it includes selecting materials with lower toxicity levels.

2. **Modularity and Repairability:**

- Designing products with modular components makes it easier to repair and upgrade individual parts, extending the product's lifespan and reducing the need for replacements.

3. **Energy Efficiency:**

- Sustainable design prioritizes energy-efficient components and systems to minimize the energy required for operation. This includes efficient lighting, heating, and cooling systems in buildings.

4. **Passive Design:**

- In architectural design, passive strategies, such as maximizing natural lighting and ventilation, are employed to reduce energy consumption for lighting and climate control.

5. **Resource Efficiency:**

- Sustainable design aims to reduce resource consumption by optimizing designs for minimal waste during manufacturing and construction.

6. **Lifecycle Assessment:**

- Similar to green computing, sustainable design involves conducting a lifecycle assessment to evaluate the environmental impact of a product or building, taking into account raw material extraction, production, transportation, use, and disposal.

7. **Certifications and Standards:**

- Adhering to sustainability standards and certifications, such as LEED (Leadership in Energy and Environmental Design) for buildings or ENERGY STAR for appliances, helps ensure that products and structures meet specific sustainability criteria.

8. **Renewable Energy Integration:**

- Sustainable design often incorporates renewable energy sources, such as solar panels or wind turbines, to generate clean energy on-site.

9. **Biophilic Design:**

- Biophilic design principles incorporate natural elements, such as green spaces and natural materials, into buildings to enhance occupant well-being and reduce the environmental impact.

Both green computing and sustainable design contribute to reducing the carbon footprint of technology and infrastructure. They promote responsible resource use, energy conservation, and a shift toward environmentally friendly practices in the IT and architectural industries. These principles are crucial for creating a more sustainable and environmentally responsible future.

Chapter 13: Emerging Trends and Future Directions

- ## Quantum Computing and Quantum Architectures

Quantum computing is a cutting-edge field of study that leverages the principles of quantum mechanics to perform computations that would be infeasible for classical computers. Quantum architectures are the physical or logical structures used to implement quantum computers. Below, I'll provide a detailed overview of quantum computing and various quantum architectures:

Quantum Computing:

1. **Quantum Bits (Qubits):**

   - Quantum computing relies on qubits, the quantum analogs of classical bits. Unlike classical bits, qubits can exist in a superposition of states, meaning they can represent both 0 and 1 simultaneously. This property enables quantum computers to perform certain calculations exponentially faster than classical computers.

2. **Quantum Entanglement:**

   - Qubits can become entangled, where the state of one qubit is dependent on the state of another, even if they are physically separated. Entanglement is a fundamental property used in quantum algorithms, such as quantum teleportation and quantum cryptography.

3. **Quantum Gates:**

   - Quantum gates are analogous to classical logic gates but operate on qubits. Common quantum gates include the Hadamard gate, CNOT gate, and T gate, among others. These gates manipulate the quantum states of qubits to perform quantum computations.

4. **Quantum Algorithms:**

   - Quantum algorithms, like Shor's algorithm and Grover's algorithm, are designed to take advantage of quantum properties to solve specific problems efficiently. For instance, Shor's algorithm can factor large numbers exponentially faster than classical algorithms, which has implications for cryptography.

5. **Quantum Error Correction:**

   - Quantum computers are highly susceptible to errors due to environmental factors like decoherence and noise. Quantum error correction codes are used to detect and correct these errors, making quantum computation more reliable.

Quantum Architectures:

1. **Circuit Model Quantum Computers:**

   - In this architecture, quantum operations are performed in a sequence of quantum gates, similar to classical circuits. Quantum circuits are composed of qubits and quantum gates and can represent various quantum algorithms.

2. **Quantum Annealers:**

- Quantum annealers, like those developed by D-Wave Systems, are specialized quantum computers designed for solving optimization problems. They use quantum annealing to find the lowest-energy configuration of a system, making them suitable for tasks like optimization and sampling.

3. **Topological Quantum Computers:**

- Topological quantum computers, based on topological qubits (e.g., anyons), are being explored as a potential architecture. They are known for their fault-tolerant properties, making them less sensitive to decoherence.

4. **Ion Trap Quantum Computers:**

- Ion trap quantum computers use electromagnetic fields to trap ions (typically qubits) and manipulate their quantum states. This architecture has been implemented by companies like IBM and Google.

5. **Superconducting Quantum Computers:**

- Superconducting qubits are typically implemented using tiny circuits of superconducting material cooled to extremely low temperatures. IBM and Google have developed superconducting quantum processors, such as IBM Q and Google's Sycamore.

6. **Photonic Quantum Computers:**

- Photonic quantum computers use photons (particles of light) as qubits. They have the advantage of being less susceptible to decoherence, but building scalable photonic quantum computers remains a challenge.

7. **Hybrid Quantum Systems:**

- Hybrid quantum systems combine quantum processors with classical components to solve complex problems. These systems leverage the strengths of both quantum and classical computing.

8. **Quantum Communication Architectures:**

- Quantum communication networks, like quantum key distribution (QKD) systems, use quantum properties for secure communication. These networks employ quantum encryption to ensure data privacy.

Quantum computing and its various architectures are still in the early stages of development, with significant challenges in terms of error correction, scalability, and practical application. Nevertheless, the potential impact of quantum computing on fields like cryptography, optimization, and materials science is substantial, and research and development in this area continue to advance rapidly.

- ## Neuromorphic Computing and Brain-Inspired Architectures

Neuromorphic computing and brain-inspired architectures are fields of research focused on designing and building computer systems that mimic the structure and function of the human brain. These technologies aim to replicate the brain's neural networks and cognitive processes, potentially leading to more efficient and powerful computing systems. Here, I'll provide a detailed overview of neuromorphic computing and brain-inspired architectures:

Neuromorphic Computing:

1. **Definition:**

   - Neuromorphic computing refers to the design of computer systems, hardware, and software that are inspired by the organization and functioning of the human brain.

2. **Neural Networks:**

   - At the heart of neuromorphic computing are artificial neural networks, which are computational models composed of interconnected nodes (neurons) that process information in a manner similar to biological neurons. These networks are capable of learning and performing tasks like pattern recognition, classification, and decision-making.

3. **Spiking Neural Networks (SNNs):**

   - Spiking neural networks are a specific type of artificial neural network that closely mimics the behavior of biological neurons. Instead of continuous firing rates, SNNs use discrete spikes or action potentials to transmit information.

4. **Hardware Accelerators:**

   - Neuromorphic computing often involves specialized hardware accelerators designed to efficiently implement neural network computations. These accelerators can be more power-efficient for certain tasks compared to traditional CPUs or GPUs.

5. **Event-Driven Processing:**

   - Neuromorphic systems typically operate in an event-driven manner, only expending energy and processing resources when specific events or changes occur in the input data. This mimics the brain's energy-efficient processing, where neurons fire only when necessary.

6. **Applications:**

   - Neuromorphic computing has applications in various fields, including robotics, image and speech recognition, sensor data processing, and neuromorphic vision systems. These systems excel at real-time processing and low-power computing.

Brain-Inspired Architectures:

1. **Memristors:**

   - Memristors are resistive switching devices that mimic the synaptic plasticity of biological synapses. They can be used as memory and storage elements in brain-inspired architectures, enabling adaptive learning and memory retention.

2. **Neuromorphic Hardware:**

   - Brain-inspired hardware architectures are designed to replicate neural processing and connectivity patterns. Hardware like neuromorphic chips or brain-inspired processors aims to provide a physical implementation of neural networks.

3. **Spiking Neuromorphic Hardware:**

- Some brain-inspired hardware, like IBM's TrueNorth chip, utilizes spiking neural network models to perform tasks such as image recognition and natural language processing efficiently.

4. **Neurosynaptic Cores:**

   - IBM's SyNAPSE project introduced neurosynaptic cores, which are specialized computing cores that emulate the behavior of neurons and synapses. These cores are used in neuromorphic hardware for cognitive computing applications.

5. **Neuromorphic Sensors:**

   - Brain-inspired architectures often incorporate neuromorphic sensors, which capture data in a manner similar to human senses. These sensors are particularly useful for robotics and autonomous systems.

6. **Neurocomputational Models:**

   - Researchers develop neurocomputational models that attempt to simulate various aspects of brain function. These models inform the design and development of brain-inspired architectures.

7. **Brain-Computer Interfaces (BCIs):**

   - Brain-inspired technologies are also used in BCIs, allowing direct communication between the brain and computers. BCIs can assist individuals with disabilities and advance research in neuroscience and neuroprosthetics.

8. **Cognitive Computing:**

   - Brain-inspired architectures play a role in cognitive computing, where systems aim to emulate human-like cognitive processes, including reasoning, problem-solving, and natural language understanding.

Neuromorphic computing and brain-inspired architectures hold promise for revolutionizing computing by enabling energy-efficient and highly parallelized processing, as well as advancing our understanding of the brain's complex functioning. Researchers and engineers continue to explore these areas for various applications in AI, robotics, neuroscience, and beyond.

- ### Edge Computing and IoT Architectures

Edge computing and IoT (Internet of Things) architectures are closely intertwined concepts that address the need for distributed and localized processing in IoT ecosystems. Here, I'll provide a detailed overview of both edge computing and IoT architectures:

Edge Computing:

1. **Definition:**

   - Edge computing is a decentralized computing paradigm that brings computation and data storage closer to the data source or "edge" of the network. Instead of sending all data to centralized cloud servers, processing occurs locally or at the edge, near the IoT devices generating the data.

2. **Latency Reduction:**

- Edge computing aims to minimize latency by processing data locally. This is critical for applications where real-time or near-real-time responses are required, such as autonomous vehicles, industrial automation, and remote medical monitoring.

3. **Bandwidth Efficiency:**

    - By processing data at the edge, only relevant or summarized information needs to be sent to the cloud, reducing the amount of data transmitted over the network. This can result in cost savings and more efficient use of network resources.

4. **Edge Devices:**

    - Edge devices, which can include IoT sensors, gateways, and edge servers, play a central role in edge computing. These devices are responsible for collecting, preprocessing, and sometimes even analyzing data before forwarding it to the cloud.

5. **Fog Computing:**

    - Fog computing is a subset of edge computing that extends the capabilities of edge devices. Fog nodes, located closer to the edge, can perform more complex processing tasks and offer additional storage and networking capabilities.

6. **Use Cases:**

    - Edge computing is used in various industries, including manufacturing, healthcare, smart cities, and agriculture. Examples include predictive maintenance in manufacturing, real-time patient monitoring in healthcare, and traffic optimization in smart cities.

7. **Security and Privacy:**

    - Edge computing can enhance security and privacy by reducing the exposure of sensitive data to the cloud. Data remains closer to the source, minimizing the risk of interception during transmission.

IoT Architectures:

1. **Device Layer:**

    - The device layer consists of IoT sensors, actuators, and devices that collect and transmit data. These devices can be simple sensors (e.g., temperature sensors) or more complex IoT endpoints (e.g., smart cameras).

2. **Communication Layer:**

    - The communication layer includes protocols and networks that enable devices to transmit data to a central point, such as an edge server or cloud. Common IoT communication protocols include MQTT, CoAP, and HTTP.

3. **Edge Layer:**

    - In the context of IoT, the edge layer consists of edge devices and gateways that preprocess data locally. Edge computing capabilities, such as data filtering, aggregation, and initial analysis, are often performed at this layer.

4. **Cloud Layer:**

- The cloud layer represents the centralized computing and storage resources typically hosted in data centers. Cloud services process and store data, enabling advanced analytics, machine learning, and long-term data storage.

5. **Analytics and Applications Layer:**

   - At this layer, data from IoT devices is processed and analyzed to derive insights and trigger actions. It includes applications, dashboards, and analytics tools that make use of the data generated by IoT devices.

6. **Security and Management Layer:**

   - Security measures, such as encryption, access control, and device management, are implemented at various layers of the IoT architecture to protect data and ensure the reliability of devices.

7. **Scalability and Interoperability:**

   - IoT architectures need to be scalable to accommodate a growing number of devices and interoperable to allow devices from different manufacturers to work together seamlessly.

8. **Real-Time and Batch Processing:**

   - Depending on the use case, IoT architectures may require real-time processing for immediate actions and batch processing for historical analysis and reporting.

9. **Hybrid Architectures:**

   - Some IoT implementations combine elements of both edge computing and cloud computing to balance the advantages of local processing and centralized data analysis.

IoT architectures and edge computing are critical components of modern connected systems, enabling the collection, analysis, and utilization of vast amounts of data generated by IoT devices. These technologies continue to evolve to meet the demands of diverse IoT applications across various industries.

- ## Ethical and Security Implications in Computer Architecture

Ethical and security implications in computer architecture are critical considerations in the design, implementation, and use of computer systems. These implications impact both the individuals and organizations that develop and use technology and society at large. Here's a detailed exploration of the ethical and security aspects in computer architecture:

Ethical Implications:

1. **Privacy Concerns:**

   - Ethical concerns related to privacy arise when computer systems collect, store, or process personal data without consent. Computer architects must consider privacy by design and incorporate data protection mechanisms into their systems.

2. **Data Ownership and Control:**

- Determining who owns and controls data in computer systems can be ethically challenging. Architectures should allow individuals to have control over their own data and know how it is being used.

3. **Transparency and Accountability:**

- Ethical design includes transparency in how algorithms work and accountability for the consequences of system behavior. Designers should make it clear how decisions are made within the architecture.

4. **Bias and Fairness:**

- Computer architectures that rely on machine learning or AI algorithms may inadvertently perpetuate biases present in training data. Ethical concerns arise when these biases result in discrimination against certain groups.

5. **Informed Consent:**

- Ethical principles require that individuals using computer systems provide informed consent regarding data collection, tracking, and profiling. Systems should clearly communicate their data practices and seek consent when necessary.

6. **Accessibility:**

- Ethical considerations include ensuring that computer architectures are accessible to individuals with disabilities. This involves designing hardware and software that accommodate various needs, such as screen readers and voice commands.

7. **Environmental Impact:**

- The ethical use of resources is vital in computer architecture. Designers should consider the environmental impact of their systems, including energy consumption and electronic waste generation.

8. **Security:**

- While security is often discussed from a technical standpoint, it also has ethical dimensions. Neglecting security measures can lead to data breaches and harm to individuals or organizations.

Security Implications:

1. **Data Security:**

- Protecting data against unauthorized access, modification, or theft is a fundamental security concern in computer architecture. Encryption, access control, and secure storage mechanisms are crucial.

2. **System Integrity:**

- Ensuring the integrity of hardware and software components is essential to prevent malicious tampering. Techniques like secure boot, code signing, and hardware security modules (HSMs) are used to establish trust.

3. **Vulnerability Management:**

- Computer architects must consider the identification and mitigation of vulnerabilities in their designs. This includes regular patching, security audits, and adherence to best practices.

4. **Network Security:**

   - Protecting networked systems against threats like unauthorized access, DDoS attacks, and eavesdropping is vital. Firewalls, intrusion detection systems (IDS), and secure communication protocols are employed.

5. **Authentication and Authorization:**

   - Proper authentication and authorization mechanisms are necessary to ensure that only authorized users or processes can access specific resources within the system.

6. **Ethical Hacking and Penetration Testing:**

   - Proactive security measures include ethical hacking and penetration testing to identify vulnerabilities before malicious actors exploit them.

7. **Incident Response:**

   - Computer architects should have plans in place for responding to security incidents. This includes monitoring for threats, incident detection, and coordinated responses.

8. **Compliance and Regulations:**

   - Security architectures must comply with legal and regulatory requirements related to data protection and cybersecurity.

9. **Supply Chain Security:**

   - Ensuring the security of components and software throughout the supply chain is vital to prevent hardware and software vulnerabilities from being introduced at various stages of production.

10. **User Education:**

    - Security is a shared responsibility, and user education is crucial. Architects should consider user-friendly security measures and provide educational resources to users.

Addressing ethical and security implications in computer architecture is an ongoing process that requires collaboration between engineers, designers, policymakers, and ethicists. By considering these factors from the early stages of design, technology can be developed and used in ways that are both responsible and secure.

Epilogue: Navigating the Digital Frontier

- ### The Ever-Evolving Landscape of Computer Architecture

The landscape of computer architecture is continually evolving to meet the growing demands of technology, industry trends, and user needs. This evolution encompasses various aspects, including hardware, software, design paradigms, and emerging technologies. Here's a detailed exploration of the ever-evolving landscape of computer architecture:

1. Moore's Law and Performance Scaling:

- Moore's Law, which predicted that the number of transistors on a microchip would double approximately every two years, has driven the continuous improvement in computing performance for several decades. However, as transistor sizes approach physical limits, the industry has had to explore new avenues for performance gains.

2. Multi-Core and Parallel Computing:

- To address the diminishing returns of single-core performance improvements, computer architectures have shifted towards multi-core processors. Modern CPUs often contain multiple cores that can execute tasks concurrently. Parallel computing has become essential for tasks like scientific simulations, data analysis, and AI.

3. Heterogeneous Computing:

- Heterogeneous computing combines different types of processing units, such as CPUs, GPUs, TPUs (Tensor Processing Units), and FPGAs (Field-Programmable Gate Arrays), to optimize performance for specific workloads. This approach is crucial for AI and deep learning applications.

4. Energy Efficiency and Power Management:

- Energy efficiency has become a top priority in computer architecture. Mobile devices, IoT sensors, and data centers all benefit from energy-efficient designs and power management techniques to extend battery life and reduce operating costs.

5. Quantum Computing:

- Quantum computing represents a groundbreaking shift in computer architecture. Quantum processors leverage the principles of quantum mechanics to perform computations that are currently impossible for classical computers, potentially revolutionizing fields like cryptography, optimization, and materials science.

6. Neuromorphic and Brain-Inspired Computing:

- Inspired by the human brain, neuromorphic computing aims to create hardware and software architectures that can process information in a manner similar to neural networks. These systems have applications in AI, robotics, and cognitive computing.

7. Edge Computing:

- Edge computing decentralizes computation and data processing by bringing computing resources closer to the data source. This approach reduces latency, conserves bandwidth, and supports real-time applications like autonomous vehicles and IoT devices.

8. Quantum-Inspired and Analog Computing:

- Quantum-inspired computing uses classical hardware to mimic certain quantum phenomena, offering some advantages over traditional computing for specific tasks. Analog computing employs continuous signals to solve mathematical problems, offering potential speed and efficiency benefits.

9. Security and Trust:

- Security considerations are integral to modern computer architecture. Hardware-level security features, like hardware security modules (HSMs) and trusted execution environments, protect against cyber threats and ensure data integrity.

10. Ethical and Green Computing: - Ethical considerations in computer architecture focus on privacy, fairness, transparency, and the responsible use of technology. Green computing emphasizes energy efficiency, sustainable design, and minimizing environmental impact.

11. Reconfigurable and Adaptive Architectures: - Reconfigurable architectures, like FPGAs, offer flexibility by allowing users to program hardware to suit specific tasks. Adaptive architectures can dynamically adjust resources based on workload demands.

12. Memory and Storage Advances: - Innovations in memory technologies, such as 3D NAND and persistent memory, have significantly increased storage capacity and data access speeds. These advancements impact both server and consumer computing.

13. Quantum-Safe Cryptography: - As quantum computers threaten classical encryption methods, computer architects are working on quantum-safe cryptographic algorithms and hardware solutions to ensure the security of data in the post-quantum era.

14. Post-Moore's Law Era: - As the semiconductor industry faces physical limits imposed by Moore's Law, computer architects must explore new technologies, such as nanotechnology, photonic computing, and beyond-CMOS devices, to sustain computational advancements.

The ever-evolving landscape of computer architecture reflects the relentless pursuit of improved performance, energy efficiency, and novel applications. Innovations in hardware, software, and design paradigms will continue to shape the future of computing, enabling breakthroughs in fields ranging from artificial intelligence and quantum computing to sustainable technology and ethical design. This evolution underscores the dynamic nature of the computing industry and its profound impact on society.

- ### Bridging Theory and Practice in Designing Computing Systems

Bridging theory and practice in designing computing systems is essential for creating technology solutions that are both effective and efficient. This process involves translating theoretical concepts and principles into practical, real-world implementations. Here's a detailed exploration of how theory and practice come together in designing computing systems:

1. Understanding the Theoretical Foundations:

- **Computer Science Fundamentals:** Start with a strong understanding of fundamental computer science principles, including algorithms, data structures, and computational theory. These theories provide the foundation for designing efficient and effective systems.

- **Domain-Specific Theories:** Depending on the application domain, you may need to delve into specific theories and models. For example, if designing a database system, understanding relational algebra and normalization theory is crucial.

2. Problem Specification and Requirements Analysis:

- **Identify the Problem:** Clearly define the problem you intend to solve with your computing system. Understand the requirements, constraints, and objectives of the project.

- **Translate Theory into Requirements:** Use theoretical knowledge to translate high-level concepts into concrete requirements. For example, if designing a distributed system, consider the theoretical principles of distributed computing to determine scalability and fault tolerance requirements.

3. System Architecture and Design:

- **Theoretical Framework:** Utilize theoretical frameworks and models to guide the architectural design of the system. This includes choosing appropriate data structures, algorithms, and software patterns.

- **Abstraction and Decomposition:** Apply theoretical principles of abstraction and decomposition to break down complex problems into manageable components. Design subsystems that address specific concerns while adhering to theoretical principles.

- **Scalability and Performance:** Use theoretical knowledge about algorithms and data structures to design for scalability and performance. Consider trade-offs and optimization techniques based on theoretical analyses.

4. Implementation and Development:

- **Programming Languages and Paradigms:** Select programming languages and paradigms that align with theoretical models. For example, functional programming languages may be suitable for systems based on mathematical or logical theories.

- **Prototyping and Testing:** Implement prototypes and conduct testing to validate theoretical assumptions and hypotheses. Testing should cover both functional and non-functional aspects, such as security and performance.

5. Optimization and Performance Tuning:

- **Algorithmic Optimization:** Use theoretical insights to optimize algorithms and data structures for efficiency. Apply techniques like algorithm analysis and complexity theory to identify bottlenecks and improve performance.

- **Profiling and Benchmarking:** Apply empirical methods to measure system performance and compare it to theoretical expectations. Identify areas where theory-practice gaps exist and make necessary adjustments.

6. Security and Reliability:

- **Theoretical Security Models:** Leverage theoretical models of security to design robust authentication, authorization, and encryption mechanisms. Ensure that the system adheres to principles like the CIA triad (confidentiality, integrity, availability).

- **Error Handling:** Implement error-handling strategies based on theoretical concepts of fault tolerance and recovery. Consider redundancy, graceful degradation, and error propagation mechanisms.

7. Validation and Verification:

- **Formal Methods:** Apply formal methods, such as model checking and formal specification languages, to rigorously verify the correctness of critical system components. Ensure that the practical implementation aligns with the theoretical specifications.

8. Documentation and Knowledge Transfer:

- **Documentation:** Maintain comprehensive documentation that explains how theoretical principles informed the design and implementation decisions. This aids in knowledge transfer and future maintenance.

9. Continuous Learning and Adaptation:

- **Stay Current:** The field of computing evolves rapidly. Continuously update your knowledge and adapt your design practices to incorporate new theoretical insights and best practices.

10. User-Centered Design:

- **User Experience (UX):** In addition to technical considerations, apply principles of UX design to ensure that the system is user-friendly and aligns with the practical needs and expectations of its users.

11. Feedback Loop:

- **Iterative Process:** Designing computing systems is often an iterative process. Gather feedback from users, monitor system performance, and make iterative improvements based on both practical experience and theoretical knowledge.

Bridging theory and practice in designing computing systems is an ongoing process that requires a deep understanding of theoretical foundations, practical constraints, and the ability to apply this knowledge effectively to solve real-world problems. This holistic approach ensures that computing systems are not only theoretically sound but also functionally robust, efficient, and user-friendly.

• Encouraging Innovation and Lifelong Learning in Technology

Encouraging innovation and lifelong learning in technology is essential in today's rapidly evolving technological landscape. Technology professionals and organizations need to foster an environment that promotes continuous growth, creativity, and adaptability. Here's a detailed exploration of how to encourage innovation and lifelong learning in the technology sector:

1. Cultivate a Culture of Curiosity and Creativity:

- **Encourage Questions:** Create an environment where asking questions is encouraged and even celebrated. Curiosity is the driving force behind innovation.

- **Open Communication:** Foster open communication channels that allow team members to share ideas and insights freely.

- **Fail Forward:** Embrace the concept of "failing forward." Encourage experimentation and view failures as learning opportunities rather than setbacks.

2. Support Continuous Learning:

- **Professional Development:** Provide opportunities and resources for employees to engage in continuous learning. This includes access to courses, workshops, and conferences.

- **Mentorship and Coaching:** Establish mentorship programs to facilitate knowledge transfer and skills development. Pair experienced professionals with those eager to learn.

- **Time for Learning:** Allocate dedicated time for employees to engage in learning activities, whether through self-study or formal training.

3. Promote Cross-Disciplinary Learning:

- **Encourage Cross-Training:** Encourage employees to explore areas outside their immediate expertise. Cross-training can lead to fresh perspectives and innovative solutions.

- **Interdisciplinary Teams:** Form interdisciplinary teams where individuals from different technical backgrounds collaborate to solve complex problems.

4. Recognize and Reward Innovation:

- **Innovation Awards:** Establish innovation awards or recognition programs to celebrate and reward creative solutions and contributions.

- **Innovation Time:** Implement "innovation time" or "hackathons" where employees are given dedicated time to work on innovative projects of their choice.

5. Create Space for Experimentation:

- **Sandbox Environments:** Set up sandbox environments or innovation labs where employees can experiment with emerging technologies without fear of disrupting production systems.

- **Prototyping:** Encourage the creation of prototypes and proof-of-concept projects to test new ideas before committing significant resources.

6. Embrace Diversity and Inclusion:

- **Diverse Teams:** Build diverse teams with members from different backgrounds, cultures, and experiences. Diverse perspectives can lead to more innovative solutions.

- **Inclusive Culture:** Foster an inclusive culture where everyone feels valued and heard, as this can inspire creativity and innovation.

7. Stay Current with Technology Trends:

- **Technology Scouting:** Stay updated on emerging technologies and trends in the industry. Technology scouting helps identify opportunities for innovation.

- **Continuous Research:** Dedicate resources to research and development efforts to explore new technologies and their potential applications.

8. Promote Intrapreneurship:

- **Intrapreneurial Programs:** Encourage employees to pursue intrapreneurial initiatives within the organization. Provide resources and support for innovative projects that align with the company's goals.

9. Encourage Networking and Collaboration:

- **Industry Conferences:** Send employees to industry conferences and events where they can network with peers, share knowledge, and gain new insights.

- **Collaborative Platforms:** Implement collaborative tools and platforms that facilitate knowledge sharing and cross-team collaboration.

10. Lead by Example:

- **Leadership Involvement:** Leadership should actively engage in lifelong learning and innovation, setting an example for the rest of the organization.

- **Support and Sponsorship:** Leaders should support and sponsor innovation initiatives and allocate resources to innovative projects.

11. Measure and Track Progress:

- **Key Performance Indicators (KPIs):** Establish KPIs to track the impact of innovation and lifelong learning efforts on the organization's performance.

- **Feedback Loops:** Collect feedback from employees to assess the effectiveness of learning and innovation programs and make necessary adjustments.

Encouraging innovation and lifelong learning is an ongoing process that requires commitment at all levels of an organization. By creating a culture of curiosity, providing opportunities for skill development, and fostering collaboration, organizations can stay at the forefront of technological advancements and empower their employees to drive innovation.

"Foundations of Computer Architecture: Unveiling the Digital Universe" offers a comprehensive exploration of the core principles and innovations in computer architecture. From digital logic and processor design to memory hierarchies, parallel processing, and emerging technologies, this book provides readers with a solid foundation in understanding how computers are structured and optimized for performance. Whether you're an aspiring computer engineer, a curious enthusiast, or a seasoned professional, this book equips you with the knowledge to unravel the intricate design of the machines that power our digital world.

Printed in Great Britain
by Amazon